Third International Workshop on Worldwide Language Service Infrastructure and Second Workshop on Open Infrastructures and Analysis Frameworks for Human Language Technologies (WLSI-OIAF4HLT 2016)

Osaka, Japan
12 December 2016

ISBN: 978-1-5108-3332-6

Preface

Language technologies and tools (hereafter called language resources) increasingly require sophisticated infrastructures to share, deploy as services, and combine to support research, development, innovation and collaboration. To address this need, several infrastructures have been recently established, including the Language Grid, the Language Application Grid, META-SHARE, DKPro, and CLARIN's Weblicht. While these infrastructures allow users to develop applications using deployed language resources/services, users are typically restricted to tools and resources available through a single infrastructure due to a lack of interoperability. The lack of interoperability among infrastructures has led to duplicated software development efforts as well as redundancy among efforts to manage language resource access, handle licensing concerns, etc.

WLSI-3/OIAF4HLT-2 focuses on the technological and institutional challenges that impact an effort to construct a worldwide interoperable language service infrastructure. It aims to bring together members of the NLP community, including operators of language service infrastructures, but also resource users, developers, and providers, in order to explore and discuss the requirements and desiderata for NLP infrastructures, as well as the opportunities and challenges for enabling interoperable communication among existing infrastructures. The combination of two previously successful workshops addressing NLP infrastructure development and interoperability reflects the recognition of the need for a global effort to achieve mutual interoperability among tools and platforms, and will bring together communities that have previously had little contact.

This volume contains 10 papers from the Third International Workshop on Worldwide Language Service Infrastructure and Second Workshop on Open Infrastructures and Analysis Frameworks for Human Language Technologies (WLSI-3/OIAF4HLT-2). The papers are categorized into three parts.

The first part introduces five language service infrastructures that combine natural language processing (NLP) components to develop a language application or analyze text data. Mohanty et al. have proposed Kathaa that enables users to design a language application as an edge-labeled directed acyclic MultiGraph with NLP components. Ide et al. have integrated a workflow system called Galaxy with their Language Application Grid platform to provide users with automated multi-step analyzes and evaluation capabilities. Castilho have analyzed 274 pre-trained models for six NLP tools and reported four potential causes of interoperability problems: encoding, tokenization, normalization, and change over time. Based on these analyses, he has introduced a new tool called Model Investigator to allow model creators to perform automatic sanity checks on their models. To address interoperability problems among language services, Murakami et al. have designed Language Service ontology that enables uses to freely bind language services to a workflow while verifying their composability. Kano have suggested a simplified API for interoperability in order for the developers to more easily employ the functions of Kachako platform.

The second part reports on language service application. Nakaguchi et al. have developed a multi-language support system for international symposiums by combining human inputters and language services on the Language Grid. Assawinjaipetch et al. have proposed complaint classification by employing deep learning techniques with word embedding.

The third part focuses on development of language resources and services, especially low-resourced languages. Aili and Mushajiang have presented how to convert Uyghur dependency Treebank to a universal dependencies version. Luong and Vu have provided a non-expert setup for Kaldi, an open source speech recognition toolkit, to develop a Vietnamese Speech Recognition System. Lastly, to construct annotated corpora, Lu et al. have evaluated an ensemble based pre-annotation approach that combines multiple existing named entity taggers and categorizes annotations into normal ones and candidate ones.

We hope this book will strongly support and encourage researchers who are willing to utilize various language services worldwide to create customized language applications and multilingual environments. We are grateful to all the participants and those who have supported this workshop.

iv

November 2016

Yohei Murakami (Kyoto University, Japan)
Donghui Lin (Kyoto University, Japan)
Nancy Ide (Vassar College)
James Pustejovsky (Brandeis University)
Workshop Co-Chairs
WLSI-3/OIAF4HLT-2

Organisers

Yohei Murakami (Kyoto University, Japan)

Donghui Lin (Kyoto University, Japan)

Nancy Ide (Vassar College, USA)

James Pustejovsky (Brandeis University, USA)

Programme Committee

Mirna Adriani (University of Indonesia, Indonesia)

Mairehaba Aili (Xinjiang University, China)

Nuria Bel (Universitat Pompeu Fabra, Spain)

Kalina Bontcheva (University of Sheffield, UK)

Nicoletta Calzolari (CNR-ILC, Italy)

Richard Eckart de Castilho (Technische Universität Darmstadt, Germany)

Christopher Cieri (LDC, USA)

Khalid Choukri (ELDA, France)

Riccardo Del Gratta (CNR-ILC, Italy)

Luca Dini (Holmes Semantic Solutions, France)

Zhiqiang Gao (Southeast University, China)

Jens Grivolla (GLiCom, Universitat Pompeu Fabra, Spain)

Hitoshi Isahara (Toyohashi University of Technology, Japan)

Toru Ishida (Kyoto University, Japan)

Yoshinobu Kano (Shizuoka University, Japan)

Monica Monachini (CNR-ILC, Italy)

Weinila Mushajiang (Xinjiang University, China)

Masayuki Otani (Kyoto University, Japan)

Stelios Piperidis (ILSP, Greece)

Vu Hai Quan (University of Natural Sciences, Vietnam National University, Vietnam)

Virach Sornlertlamvanich (SIIT, Thailand)

Andrejs Vasiljevs (Tilde, Latvia)

Table of Contents

Conference Program

Monday, December 12, 2016

9:00–9:10   **Opening**

9:10–10:40   **Language Service Infrastructure 1**

9:10–9:40   *Kathaa : NLP Systems as Edge-Labeled Directed Acyclic MultiGraphs*
Sharada Mohanty, Nehal J Wani, Manish Srivastava and Dipti Sharma

9:40–10:10   *LAPPS/Galaxy: Current State and Next Steps*
Nancy Ide, Keith Suderman, Eric Nyberg, James Pustejovsky and Marc Verhagen

10:10–10:40   *Automatic Analysis of Flaws in Pre-Trained NLP Models*
Richard Eckart de Castilho

10:40–11:00   **Coffee Break**

11:00–12:00   **Language Service Application**

11:00–11:30   *Combining Human Inputters and Language Services to provide Multi-language support system for International Symposiums*
Takao Nakaguchi, Masayuki Otani, Toshiyuki Takasaki and Toru Ishida

11:30–12:00   *Recurrent Neural Network with Word Embedding for Complaint Classification*
panuwat assawinjaipetch, Kiyoaki Shirai, Virach Sornlertlamvanich and Sanparith
Marukata

12:00–13:30   **Lunch**

13:30–15:00   **Language Resources and Services**

13:30–14:00   *Universal dependencies for Uyghur*
marhaba eli, Weinila Mushajiang, Tuergen Yibulayin, Kahaerjiang Abiderexiti and
Yan Liu

14:00–14:30   *A non-expert Kaldi recipe for Vietnamese Speech Recognition System*
Hieu-Thi Luong and Hai-Quan Vu

14:30–15:00   *Evaluating Ensemble Based Pre-annotation on Named Entity Corpus Construction
in English and Chinese*
Tingming Lu, Man Zhu, Zhiqiang Gao and Yaocheng Gui

15:00–15:50   **Demo Session and Coffee Break**

15:50–16:50   **Language Service Infrastructure 2**

15:50–16:20   *An Ontology for Language Service Composability*
Yohei Murakami, Takao Nakaguchi, Donghui Lin and Toru Ishida

16:20–16:50   *Between Platform and APIs: Kachako API for Developers*
Yoshinobu Kano

16:50–17:00   Closing

Kathaa : NLP Systems as Edge-Labeled Directed Acyclic MultiGraphs

Sharada Prasanna Mohanty[1,2,3]**, Nehal J Wani**[1]**,
Manish Srivastava**[1]**, Dipti Misra Sharma**[1]

[1] LTRC, International Institute of Information Technology, Hyderabad
[2] School of Computer and Communication Sciences , EPFL, Switzerland
[3] School of Life Sciences, EPFL, Switzerland
sharada.mohanty@epfl.ch, nehal.wani@research.iiit.ac.in
{m.shrivastava, dipti}@iiit.ac.in

Abstract

We present **Kathaa**, an Open Source web-based Visual Programming Framework for Natural Language Processing (NLP) Systems. Kathaa supports the design, execution and analysis of complex NLP systems by visually connecting NLP components from an easily extensible Module Library. It models NLP systems an edge-labeled Directed Acyclic MultiGraph, and lets the user use publicly co-created modules in their own NLP applications irrespective of their technical proficiency in Natural Language Processing. Kathaa exposes an intuitive web based Interface for the users to interact with and modify complex NLP Systems; and a precise Module definition API to allow easy integration of new state of the art NLP components. Kathaa enables researchers to *publish their services* in a standardized format to enable the masses to use their services out of the box. The vision of this work is to pave the way for a system like Kathaa, to be the *Lego blocks* of NLP Research and Applications. As a practical use case we use Kathaa to visually implement the Sampark Hindi-Panjabi Machine Translation Pipeline and the Sampark Hindi-Urdu Machine Translation Pipeline, to demonstrate the fact that Kathaa can handle really complex NLP systems while still being intuitive for the end user.

1 Introduction

Natural Language Processing systems are inherently very complex, and their design is heavily tied up with their implementation. There is a huge diversity in the way the individual components of the complex system consume, process and spit out information. Many of the components also have associated services which mostly are really hard to replicate and/or setup. Hence, most researchers end up writing their own in-house methods for gluing the components together, and in many cases, own in-house re-implementations of the individual components, often inefficient re-implementations.

On top of that, most of the popular NLP components make many assumptions about the technical proficiency of the user who will be using those components. All of these factors clubbed together shut many potential users out of the whole ecosystem of NLP systems, and hence many potentially creative applications of these components. With Kathaa, we aim to separate the design and implementation layers of Natural Language Processing systems, and efficiently pack every component into consistent and reusable black-boxes which can be made to interface with each other through an intuitive visual interface, irrespective of the software environment in which the components reside, and irrespective of the technical proficiency of the user using the system. Kathaa builds on top of numerous ideas explored in the academia around Visual Programming Languages in general (Green and Petre, 1996) (Shu, 1988) (Myers, 1990), and also on Visual Programming Languages in the context of NLP (Cunningham et al., 1997). In a previous demonstration (Mohanty et al., 2016) at NAACL-HLT-2016, we showcased many of the features of Kathaa, and because of the general interest in Kathaa, we are now making an attempt to more formally model Kathaa in this paper.

Proceedings of WLSI/OIAF4HLT,
pages 1–10, Osaka, Japan, December 12 2016.

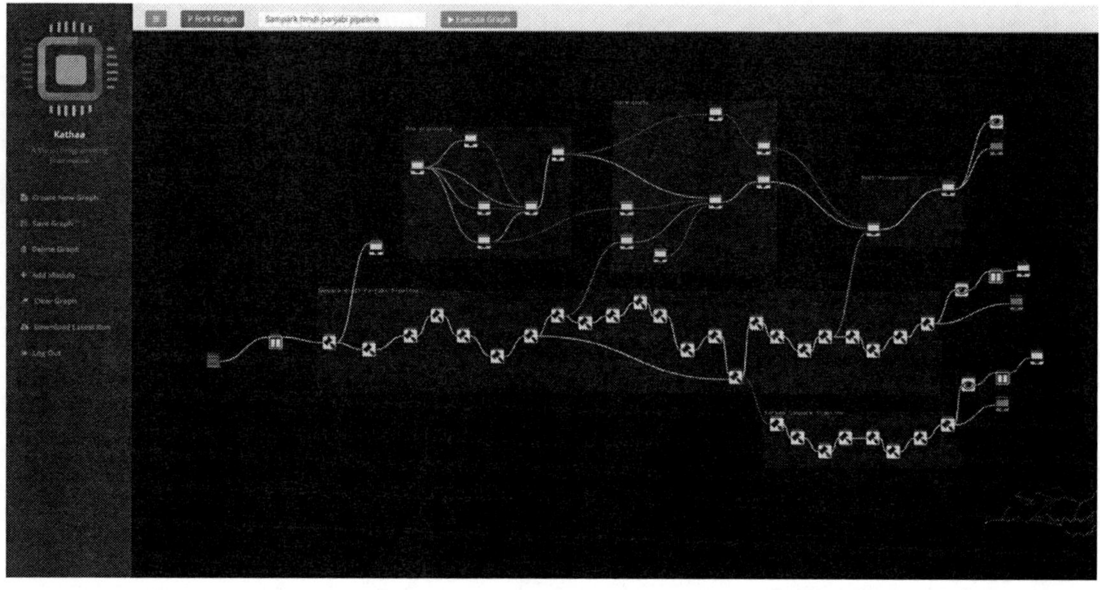

Figure 1: Example of a Hindi-Panjabi Machine Translation System, visually implemented using Kathaa.

2 Kathaa Modules

Kathaa Modules are the basic units of computation in the proposed Visual Programming Framework. They consume the input(s) across multiple input ports, process them, and finally pass on their output(s) across the many output ports they might have. The user has access to a whole array of such modules with different utilities via the Kathaa Module Library. The user can connect together these modules in any combination as he pleases (as long as the connections between the said modules are compatible with each other). The user also has the ability to tinker with the functionality of a particular module in real time by using an embedded code editor in the Kathaa Visual Interface during or before the execution of the Kathaa Graph. The inspiration behind Kathaa Modules comes from the Black Box approach in Integrated Digital Circuits, where rather complex combinations of Logic Gates are arranged in complex arrangements to get a desired behavior from the circuit, and then finally the overall arrangement is treated as a black box. The 'users' of this particular Integrated Circuit or 'chip', just need to refer to the Data Sheet of the chip for the input and output specifications to be able to use the said chip for designing more complex and high-level circuits.

Kathaa Modules aim to be the Integrated Circuits for NLP, which can be mixed and matched together to create interesting NLP Applications while hiding the complex implementation details in a black box.

2.1 Kathaa Data Blobs and Kathaa Data Sub Blobs

The input received at a particular input port, or the output generated at a particular output port of a module is always a collection of **kathaa-data-sub-blob**s. Each input port receives exactly the same number (as the rest of the input ports) of *kathaa-data-sub-blob*s, and similarly each output port holds exactly the same number (as the rest of the output ports) of *kathaa-data-sub-blob*s. A **kathaa-data-blob** is also a collection of *kathaa-data-sub-blob*s, but every *kathaa-data-blob* contains just one *kathaa-data-sub-blob* from each of the input ports (or the output ports, depending on if its a kathaa-data-blob at the Input Layer of the module or at the Output Layer of the module). The n-th *kathaa-data-sub-blob* of all the input ports, contributes to the n-th Input *kathaa-data-blob* of the Module Instance; similarly, the m-th *kathaa-data-sub-blob* of all the output ports, contributes to the m-th Output *kathaa-data-blob* of the Module Instance. A Kathaa Module has the capability to process multiple *kathaa-data-blobs* in parallel by spawning multiple instances of the same module during execution. The concept of numerous data blobs spread across multiple input ports (or output ports) enables us to efficiently empower module writers to leverage from the inherent parallelizability in tasks performed by numerous NLP components. For example, some modules are parallelizable at the level of sentences, so if we have multiple sentences as inputs to this module, all those sentences are passed as different *kathaa-data-blob*s so that the framework can parallelize their processing depending on the availability of resources. Similarly, other modules could expect parallelizability at the level of words, or phrases or even a whole discourse. The *kathaa-data-blobs* were very much inspired by the data-blobs used in Caffe (Jia et al., 2014).

2.2 Formal definition of Kathaa Modules

A Kathaa Module can very simply be modeled as :

$$F(IP) = OP \tag{1}$$

where, $F()$ refers to the overall function the Module represents; IP refers to the overall Input object that the Module receives; and OP refers to the overall Output object that the Module produces.

The inputs and outputs for Kathaa Modules are spread across multiple input ports and output ports, so IP and OP can basically be represented as a collection of input and output values across all the input and output ports

$$IP = [IP_0, IP_1, \ldots\ldots\ldots, IP_{N-1}, IP_N] \qquad OP = [OP_0, OP_1, \ldots\ldots\ldots, OP_{M-1}, OP_M] \tag{2}$$

where IP_n refers to the input received on input port n, where $n \in [0, N)$; and N is the maximum number of Input Ports supported by Kathaa for Kathaa Modules; OP_m refers to the output generated on output port m, where $m \in [0, M)$; and M is the maximum number of Output Ports supported by Kathaa for Kathaa Modules.

Every input received on any of the input ports IP_n or every output generated on any of the output ports OP_m is but a collection of *kathaa-data-sub-blobs*, which are the basic primitives of data handling in Kathaa. So, IP_n and OP_m can be further represented as :

$$IP_n = [IP_{n,0}, IP_{n,1}, \ldots\ldots\ldots, IP_{n,X-1}, IP_{n,X}] \qquad OP_m = [OP_{m,0}, OP_{m,1}, \ldots\ldots\ldots, OP_{m,Y-1}, OP_{m,Y}] \tag{3}$$

Where X and Y refer to the number of *kathaa-data-sub-blob*s in each of the ports in the Input and Output layers respectively.

Now by substituting Equation 3 in Equation 2, we can represent IP and OP as a combined input and output matrices as follows :

$$IP = \begin{bmatrix} IP_{0,0} & IP_{0,1} & .. & P_{0,X-1} & IP_{0,X} \\ IP_{1,0} & IP_{1,1} & .. & P_{1,X-1} & IP_{1,X} \\ . & . & .. & . & . \\ . & . & .. & . & . \\ IP_{N-1,0} & IP_{N-1,1} & .. & IP_{N-1,X-1} & IP_{N-1,X} \\ IP_{N,0} & IP_{N,1} & .. & IP_{N,X-1} & IP_{N,X} \end{bmatrix} \qquad OP = \begin{bmatrix} OP_{0,0} & OP_{0,1} & .. & OP_{0,Y-1} & OP_{0,Y} \\ OP_{1,0} & OP_{1,1} & .. & OP_{1,Y-1} & OP_{1,Y} \\ . & . & .. & . & . \\ . & . & .. & . & . \\ OP_{M-1,0} & OP_{M-1,1} & .. & OP_{M-1,Y-1} & OP_{M-1,Y} \\ OP_{M,0} & OP_{M,1} & .. & OP_{M,Y-1} & OP_{M,Y} \end{bmatrix} \tag{4}$$

where $IP_{n,x}$ refers to the x-th *kathaa-data-sub-blob* on the n-th Input Port of the kathaa module; and $OP_{m,y}$ refers to the y-th *kathaa-data-sub-blob* on the m-th Output Port of the kathaa module.

Now lets define $IP_{*,k}$ as the collection of the k-th corresponding *kathaa-data-sub-blob*s across all the Input ports; and $OP_{*,p}$ as the collection of the p-th corresponding *kathaa-data-sub-blob*s across all the Output ports. So,

$$IP_{*,k} = [IP_{0,k}, IP_{1,k}, \ldots\ldots\ldots, IP_{N-1,k}, IP_{N,k}] \qquad OP_{*,k} = [OP_{0,k}, OP_{1,k}, \ldots\ldots\ldots, OP_{M-1,k}, OP_{M,k}] \tag{5}$$

$IP_{*,k}$ and $OP_{*,k}$ represent a single *kathaa-data-blob* in the Input and the Output layers respectively. Figure 2 shows the organization of *kathaa-data-blobs*, *kathaa-data-sub-blobs* and Input and Output Port values in the Combined Input and Output Matrices as defined in Equation 4.

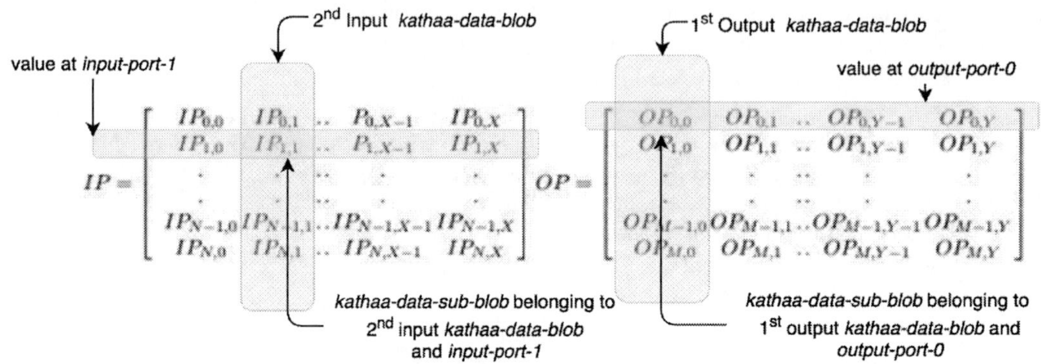

Figure 2: Organization of *kathaa-data-blobs*, *kathaa-data-sub-blobs* and Input and Output Port values in the Combined Input and Output Matrices as defined in Equation 4.

By using Equation 5, we can represent IP and OP as a collection of *kathaa-data-blob*s in the Input and Output layers as follows :

$$
\begin{aligned}
IP &= [(IP_{*,0})^T, (IP_{*,1})^T, \ldots\ldots\ldots, (IP_{*,X-1})^T, (IP_{*,X})^T] \\
OP &= [(OP_{*,0})^T, (OP_{*,1})^T, \ldots\ldots\ldots, (OP_{*,Y-1})^T, (OP_{*,Y})^T]
\end{aligned}
\tag{6}
$$

Finally, substituting Equation 6 in Equation 1, we obtain :

$$
\begin{aligned}
F([(IP_{*,0})^T, (IP_{*,1})^T, \ldots\ldots\ldots, (IP_{*,X-1})^T, (IP_{*,X})^T]) = \\
[(OP_{*,0})^T, (OP_{*,1})^T, \ldots\ldots\ldots, (OP_{*,Y-1})^T, (OP_{*,Y})^T]
\end{aligned}
\tag{7}
$$

For easy readability, we can define the substitutions $IB_i = (IP_{*,i})^T$ and $OB_i = (OP_{*,i})^T$, which represent an Input *kathaa-data-blob* and an Output *kathaa-data-blob* respectively. We can now rewrite Equation 7 as :

$$
F([IB_0, IB_1, \ldots\ldots\ldots, IB_{X-1}, IB_X]) = [OB_0, OB_1, OB_2, \ldots\ldots\ldots, OB_{Y-1}, OB_Y]
\tag{8}
$$

which captures the crux of how Kathaa Modules manipulate data, by consuming a collection of *kathaa-data-blob*s, and finally spitting out a bunch of *kathaa-data-blob*s as Output.

2.3 Types of Kathaa Modules

2.3.1 Kathaa General Modules

Kathaa General Modules are the class of Kathaa Modules which output the exact same number of *kathaa-data-blobs* as the number of *kathaa-data-blobs* in their Input Layer. Or more formally, in case of Kathaa General Modules, we will have $X = Y$ in Equation 8. As every Input *kathaa-data-blobs* independently maps to a single Output *kathaa-data-blobs*, we can imagine a function $f()$ which processes a single Input *kathaa-data-blobs*, to produce the corresponding Output *kathaa-data-blobs*.

$$
\begin{aligned}
F([IB_0, IB_1, \ldots\ldots\ldots, IB_{X-1}, IB_X]) &= [f(IB_0), f(IB_1), \ldots\ldots\ldots, f(IB_{X-1}), f(IB_X)] \\
&= [OB_0, OB_1, \ldots\ldots\ldots, OB_{X-1}, OB_X]
\end{aligned}
\tag{9}
$$

Kathaa General Modules are the most common type of Kathaa Modules, and they are defined simply by defining the single function $f()$ which takes a single *kathaa-data-blob* as input, and finally returns a single *kathaa-data-blob* as output. The *kathaa-orchestrator* internally deals with the spawning of multiple instances of the said function $f()$ and processing all the Input *kathaa-data-blob*s in parallel, and then aggregating and writing their output as a collection of Output *kathaa-data-blob*s. The idea is that module developers just have to focus on the basic functionality of their module, and the efficient parallelized execution of the same is automatically dealt by the framework, making it much easier for developers to get started with writing really powerful modules for Kathaa. To help developers get started, we also have a very flexible implementation of a `Custom Module` (Mohanty, 2016d) which can act as a quick starting point when defining Kathaa General Modules.

2.3.2 Kathaa Blob Adapters

Kathaa Blob Adapters, on the other hand, are a class of Kathaa Modules, which are provided with all the blobs from the Input Layer at the same time, and they have the ability to modify the number of blobs and pass it over to their output layer. They give the user a more fine grained control over the parallelizability of different parts of their Kathaa Graphs by varying the number of *kathaa-data-blob*s flowing through a particular point in the graph. More formally, Kathaa Blob Adapters are all the classes of Kathaa Modules where $X \neq Y$ in Equation 8. As a use case for Kathaa Blob Adapters, we can imagine a Kathaa Graph which receives a whole discourse as a single *kathaa-data-blob*, and it might benefit from processing the sentences parallely, and it could use a `Line Splitter` (Mohanty, 2016f) to split the whole discourse which was passed on as a single *kathaa-data-blob* into multiple *kathaa-data-blob*s each representing a single sentence, and when finally the user desired processing of the individual sentences are complete, a `Line Aggregator` (Mohanty, 2016e) could aggregate the processed sentences again into a single *kathaa-data-blob*. Similar kathaa-blob-adapters could be implemented to deal with splitting and aggregation of *kathaa-data-blob*s at the level of words, phrases,etc. For example, in contrast to the example cited above, if we are dealing certain language processing tasks which are inherently not parallalizable after a certain level of granularity, like, for e.g. Anaphora Resolution, Multi Document Summarisation, etc, the user will have to use an appropriate kathaa-blob-adapter, to make sure that all the information that is required for the particular task is available as a single *kathaa-data-blob*. In the case of Anaphora Resolution, a single *kathaa-data-blob* will contain a string of N sentences, and in the case of Multi Document Summarisation, a single *kathaa-data-blobs* will contain a string of M Documents.

2.3.3 Kathaa User Intervention Module

During the execution of a Kathaa Graph, the Kathaa Orchestrator ensures that the execution of a particular Kathaa Module Instance starts only after all its dependencies complete their execution and write their output. But in some NLP systems, the overall execution of the system might have to halt for some kind of user feedback. Like in the case of resource creation, where for example, you might want to start with a bunch of sentences, parse them using an available parser module, and then you would want to add Anaphora annotations by a human annotator (Sangal and Sharma, 2001). In that case, a **Kathaa User Intervention** Module can be used, where the overall execution at the particular Kathaa Module in the Kathaa Graph pauses till the user modifies the *kathaa-data-blobs* as she pleases and then resumes the execution at the said node. Internally, in case of Kathaa User Intervention Module, the Kathaa Orchestrator simply copies all the *kathaa-data-blobs* from the Input Layer to the Output Layer, and lets the user edit the Output Layer of the module through the Kathaa Visual Interface; and finally adds a User Feedback from the Kathaa Visual Interface as one of the dependencies of the Module. Kathaa Core Module group implements a `User Intervention` (Mohanty, 2016g) module, which can be used for the described use case in Kathaa Graphs.

2.3.4 Kathaa Resource Module

Kathaa Resource Modules are the class of Kathaa Modules which do not do any processing of the data, but instead they store and provide a corpus of text which can be used by any of the modules in the whole graph during execution. They do not have any Inputs, and they start executing right at the beginning of execution of the parent Kathaa Graph. More formally, they are the class of Kathaa Modules where $X = 0$ and $Y > 0$ in Equation 8.

2.3.5 Kathaa Evaluation Module

The aim of Kathaa is to provide an intuitive environment not only for prototyping and deployment but also debugging and analysis of NLP systems. Hence, we include a class of modules called as **Kathaa Evaluation Modules** which very much like kathaa-blob-adapters receive all the blobs across all the input ports, do some analysis and spit out the results into the output ports. While in principle, this a subset of kathaa-blob-adapters, these modules enjoy a separate category among Kathaa Modules because of their utility in debugging and analyzing NLP systems. We implement a sample *Classification Evaluator* (Mohanty, 2016c) to help researchers quickly come up with easy to visualize confusion matrices to aid them in evaluating the performance of any of their subsystems. This could act as a starting point for easily implementing any other Evaluation Modules.

2.4 Kathaa Module Services

Most popular NLP Components work in completely different software environments, and hence standardizing the interaction between all of them is a highly challenging task. Kathaa can allow every module to define an optional service by referencing a publicly available *docker container* in the module definition. Kathaa can deal with the life-cycle management of the referenced containers on a configurable set of Host Machines. The corresponding kathaa-modules function definition then acts as a light weight wrapper around this service. This finally enables different research groups to **publish their service** in a consistent and reusable way, such that it fits nicely in the Kathaa Module ecosystem.

2.5 Kathaa Module Packaging and Distribution

By design, the definition of Kathaa Modules is completely decoupled from the actual code base of the Kathaa Framework. The idea was to facilitate the possibility of a large community of independent and unsupervised contributors and a swarm of community contributed modules which would ultimately be available by a simple to use Kathaa-Package-Manager. While the Kathaa-Package-Manager is not yet implemented, we believe it would be pretty trivial to implement the same because of the way Kathaa Modules are designed. A set of related Kathaa Modules reside as a Kathaa Module Group in a publicly accessible `git` Repository, and the Kathaa Framework downloads and loads these Modules on the fly just by referencing their publicly accessible `URI` in the overall configuration file. Detailed documentation on the definition, packaging and distribution of Kathaa Modules along with a list and description of all the available Kathaa Modules can be found online at : *Kathaa Module Packaging and Distribution* (Mohanty, 2016b).

3 Kathaa Graph

A Kathaa Graph is an edge-labeled Directed Acyclic MultiGraph of 'instances' of Kathaa Modules, with Edges connecting one or more Output Ports of one instance of a Kathaa Module to one or more Input Ports of an instance of the same or different Kathaa Module. A Kathaa Graph can have multiple instances of the same Kathaa Module at different positions in the graph, and also with different configurations of the said instances. Each Module Instance maintains its own state, and there can be multiple directed edges between any two Module Instances. We start by defining a few key variables:

- M_k represents a Kathaa Module Instance, where $k \in [0, K)$ and K is the total number of Kathaa Module Instances in a Kathaa Graph G.
- $\psi(M_k)$ represents the state of a Kathaa Module Instance, where state being all configurable parameters of the Module, a copy of the data present at all the Input and the Output ports and the definition of the associated computational function.
- $\tau(M_k)^I$ represents the set of all input ports of the Kathaa Module Instance M_k
- $|\tau(M_k)^I|$ represents the cardinality of the set $\tau(M_k)^I$ and hence represents the total number of Input Ports in the Module Instance M_k
- $\tau(M_k)_i^I$ represents the i-th input port of the Kathaa Module Instance M_k
- $\eta(\tau(M_k)_i^I)$ represents the total number of incoming edges into the i-th input port of the Kathaa Module Instance M_k
- $\tau(M_k)^O$ represents the set of all output ports of the Kathaa Module Instance M_k
- $|\tau(M_k)^O|$ represents the cardinality of the set $\tau(M_k)^O$ and hence represents the total number of Output Ports in the Module Instance M_k

- $\tau(M_k)_j^O$ represents the j-th output port of the Kathaa Module Instance M_k
- $\eta(\tau(M_k)_j^O)$ represents the total number of outgoing edges from the j-th output port of the Kathaa Module Instance M_k

$$\tag{10}$$

We define a Kathaa Graph G as an ordered pair of its vertices V and edges E:

$$G = (V, E) \tag{11}$$

The Vertices of a Kathaa Graph are composed of Kathaa Module Instances, so we can write

$$V = \{M_k | k \in [0, K)\} \tag{12}$$

There can be multiple edges between two Nodes in a Kathaa Graph, for example when you add a directed edge between the output-port-1 of a Kathaa Module instance M_1 to the input-port-1 of another Kathaa Module instance M_2. Then you add another directed edge between the output-port-2 of the Kathaa Module Instance M_1 to the input-port-2 of the Kathaa Module instance M_2. Or more formally, Kathaa Graphs can have parallel edges.

So we define an Edge e in a Kathaa Graph G as an ordered 3-tuple :

$$e = (s, t, L) \tag{13}$$

Where, s ($s \in V$) is the Source Node of the edge; t ($t \in V$) is the Target Node of the edge, and L is the edge-label of the edge e which is represented as an ordered tuple

$$L = (s_{OP}, t_{IP}) \tag{14}$$

- s_{OP} refers to the output port of the Source Node of the edge e. And $s_{OP} \in \tau(s)^O$
- t_{IP} refers to the input port of the Target Node of the edge e. And $t_{IP} \in \tau(t)^I$

Substituting Equation 14 in Equation 13 we obtain :

$$e = (s, t, (s_{OP}, t_{IP})) \tag{15}$$

Now the set of edges E of the Kathaa Graph G can defined as :

$$E = \{(s, t, (s_{OP}, t_{IP})) \mid s, t \in V \wedge s \neq t \wedge S_{OP} \in \tau(s)^O \wedge t_{IP} \in \tau(t)^I \wedge \kappa(s_{OP}, t_{IP}) \wedge \eta(t_{IP}) = 1\} \tag{16}$$

Where, s, t are defined in Equation 13; s_{OP}, t_{IP} are defined in Equation 14; $\tau()^O$ and $\tau()^I$ and $\eta()$ are defined in Equation 10; and $\kappa(s_{OP}, t_{IP})$ refers to a boolean function which determines the compatibility of a particular Input port and Output port pair based on meta structure definition of the corresponding modules.

The conditions in Equation 16 represent some of the key properties of a Kathaa Graph. $s, t \in V$ asserts that both the Source Node and the Target Node have to be from the set of Nodes or the Module Instances in the Kathaa Graph. $s \neq t$ asserts that self loops are not allowed in a Kathaa Graph, so the Source Node and the Target Node in a Kathaa Graph cannot be the same. $S_{OP} \in \tau(s)^O$ asserts that the Output Port from the Source Node that is associated with an edge has to be a valid Output Port from the set of Output Ports of the Source Node. $t_{IP} \in \tau(t)^I$ asserts that the Input Port from the Target Node that is associated with an edge has to be a valid Input Port from the set of Output Ports of the Target Node. $\kappa(s_{OP}, t_{IP})$ asserts that the Output Port from the Source Node and the Input Port at the Target Node have to be compatible with each other based on the meta structure definition of the Source and Target Nodes. $\eta(t_{IP}) = 1$ asserts that there can be only a single edge that can be associated with an Input Port of any Module Instance in the Kathaa Graph. Now, Equation 16 defines E and Equation 12 defines V, hence we can use them in Equation 11 to finally be able to formally define a Kathaa Graph G.

4 Kathaa Orchestrator

Kathaa Orchestrator obtains the structure of the Kathaa Graph and the initial state of the execution initiator modules from the Kathaa Visual Interface, and then it efficiently orchestrates the execution of the graph depending on the nature and state of the modules, while dealing with process parallelisms, module dependencies, etc under the hood. The execution of a Kathaa Graph starts by collecting all the Nodes in the Kathaa Graph from which it should start the execution. In the case that the Visual Interface provides a Module Instance to begin execution from, the Kathaa Graph starts execution from just that Node, else it collects all the `sentence_input` nodes and the `resource` nodes. The collected nodes are simply queued in a global Job Queue. A background process, in the meantime, listens on the Job Queue, and whenever a Job is added to the queue, it tries to execute the Job on any of the available resources. The execution of the Job starts by trying to execute the actual function associated with the particular Node, and if its successful, it passes the data along all its outgoing edges to the designated input ports of module instances further along the graph, and then finally returns the obtained result object. A Job Complete event handler is called with the final result (or the exception in case of errors), and the Job Complete event handler passes along the data to the Visual Interface to update the state of the graph in the Visual Interface and provide the user with the result associated with the Module or the actual exception and the error message to help the user debug the particular Kathaa Graph. Detailed documentation on Kathaa Orchestrator can be found at : *Kathaa Orchestrator* (Mohanty, 2016a).

5 Kathaa Visual Interface

Kathaa Interface lets the user design any complex NLP system as an edge-labeled Directed Acyclic MultiGraph with the Kathaa Module Instances as nodes, and edges representing the flow of *kathaa-data-blobs* between them. Users have the option to not only execute any such graph, but also interact with it in real time by changing both the state and functionality of any of the module right from within the interface. It can be a really useful aid in debugging complex systems, as it lets the User easily visualize and modify the flow of kathaa-data-blobs across the whole Kathaa Graph. Apart from that, it also encourages code-reuse by lettings users 'Fork' a graph, or 'Remix' the designs of NLP systems to come up with better and adapted versions of the same systems. Figure 1 shows the visual implementation of a Hindi Panjabi Machine Translation system in the Kathaa Visual Interface.

6 Use Cases

Kathaa, as a Visual Programming Framework was developed with Sampark Machine Translation System as a use case. We ported all the modules of the *Hindi-Panjabi* (Mohanty, 2016h) and *Hindi-Urdu* (Mohanty, 2016i) Translation Pipelines of Sampark Machine Translation System(SAM, 2016) into Kathaa. We then demonstrated the use of Kathaa in creation of NLP Resources by the use of Kathaa User Intervention modules, and also moved on to demonstrate visual analysis of different classification approaches by using the Kathaa-Classification-Evaluation module. We are currently also exploring the use of Kathaa in classrooms to help students interact with and design complex NLP systems with a much lower barrier to entry. All these example Kathaa Graphs are the seed Graphs that are included in the repository, and can be used out of the box. It is important to note that these use cases that we managed to explore are only the tip of the iceberg when it comes to what is possible using a framework like Kathaa. One of the key features in Kathaa which enables for it to be used in a whole range of use cases is the easy extensibility. The Kathaa Module Definition API, enables the user of the system to theoretically define any function as a Kathaa Module. Also, Kathaa internally works using event triggers, hence making it a practical possibility to define modules which may run for days or weeks, quite helpful when exploring Kathaa for use cases where the user might want to define a Kathaa Module which trains a model based on some pre-processed data. The NPM (Tilkov and Vinoski, 2010) inspired packaging system, is again something which we believe can help with large scale adoption of a system like Kathaa. It paves the way for a public contributed repository of NLP components, all of which can be mashed together in any desired combination. The ability to optionally package individual services using Docker Containers also helps make a strong case when pitching for the possibility of a large public contributed repository of NLP components. These are a few things which set Kathaa apart from already existing systems like LAPPS Grid (Ide et al., 2014), ALVEO (Cassidy et al., 2014) where the easy extensibility of the system is a major bottleneck in its large scale adoption. The inter-operability between existing systems is also of key importance, and the design of Kathaa accommodates for its easy adaptation to be used along with other similar system. The assumption, of course, is that a wrapper Kathaa Module has to be designed for each target system using the Kathaa Module Definition API. The wrapper modules would be completely decoupled from the Kathaa Core codebase, and hence can be designed and implemented by anyone just like any other Kathaa Module.

A demonstration video of many features and use cases of Kathaa is also available to view at :

`https://youtu.be/woK5x0NmrUA`

7 Conclusion

We demonstrate an open source web based Visual Programming Framework for NLP Systems, and make it available for everyone to use under a MIT License. We hope our efforts can, in some way, catalyze more new and creative applications of NLP components, and enables an increased number of researchers to more comfortably tinker with and modify complex NLP Systems.

Acknowledgements

The first real world implementation of a Kathaa Graph was achieved by porting numerous modules from Sampark MT system developed during the "Indian Language to Indian Language Machine translation" (ILMT) consortium project funded by the TDIL program of Department of Electronics and Information Technology (DeitY), Govt. of India. Kathaa is built with numerous open source tools and libraries, an (almost) exhaustive list of which is available in the Github Repository of the project, and we would like to thank each and every contributor to all those projects.

References

Steve Cassidy, Dominique Estival, Tim Jones, Peter Sefton, Denis Burnham, Jared Burghold, et al. 2014. The alveo virtual laboratory: A web based repository api.

Hamish Cunningham, Kevin Humphreys, Robert Gaizauskas, and Yorick Wilks. 1997. Gate - a general architecture for text engineering. In *Proceedings of the Fifth Conference on Applied Natural Language Processing: Descriptions of System Demonstrations and Videos*, pages 29–30, Washington, DC, USA, March. Association for Computational Linguistics.

Thomas R. G. Green and Marian Petre. 1996. Usability analysis of visual programming environments: A 'cognitive dimensions' framework. *J. Vis. Lang. Comput.*, 7(2):131–174.

Nancy Ide, James Pustejovsky, Christopher Cieri, Eric Nyberg, Di Wang, Keith Suderman, Marc Verhagen, and Jonathan Wright. 2014. The language application grid. In *LREC*, pages 22–30.

Yangqing Jia, Evan Shelhamer, Jeff Donahue, Sergey Karayev, Jonathan Long, Ross Girshick, Sergio Guadarrama, and Trevor Darrell. 2014. Caffe: Convolutional architecture for fast feature embedding. In *Proceedings of the 22Nd ACM International Conference on Multimedia*, MM '14, pages 675–678, New York, NY, USA. ACM.

Sharada Prasanna Mohanty, Nehal J. Wani, Manish Shrivastava, and Dipti Misra Sharma. 2016. Kathaa: A visual programming framework for NLP applications. In *Proceedings of the Demonstrations Session, NAACL HLT 2016, The 2016 Conference of the North American Chapter of the Association for Computational Linguistics: Human Language Technologies, San Diego California, USA, June 12-17, 2016*, pages 92–96.

Sharada Prasanna Mohanty. 2016a. Kathaa Documentation : Kathaa Orchestrator. `https://github.com/kathaa/kathaa/blob/master/docs/kathaa-orchestrator.pdf`. [Online; accessed 16-October-2016].

Sharada Prasanna Mohanty. 2016b. Kathaa Documentation : Module Packaging and Distribution. `https://github.com/kathaa/kathaa/blob/master/docs/ModulePackagingAndDistribution.pdf`. [Online; accessed 16-October-2016].

Sharada Prasanna Mohanty. 2016c. Kathaa Module : Classification Evaluator. https://git.io/vV40f. [Online; accessed 16-October-2016].

Sharada Prasanna Mohanty. 2016d. Kathaa Module : Custom Module. https://git.io/vV4Rp. [Online; accessed 16-October-2016].

Sharada Prasanna Mohanty. 2016e. Kathaa Module : Line Aggregator. https://git.io/vV40v. [Online; accessed 16-October-2016].

Sharada Prasanna Mohanty. 2016f. Kathaa Module : Line Splitter. https://git.io/vV4Rj. [Online; accessed 16-October-2016].

Sharada Prasanna Mohanty. 2016g. Kathaa Module : User Intervention. https://git.io/vV40U. [Online; accessed 16-October-2016].

Sharada Prasanna Mohanty. 2016h. Kathaa Module Group : Sampark Hindi Panjabi Translation Pipeline Modules. https://github.com/kathaa/hindi-panjabi-modules. [Online; accessed 16-October-2016].

Sharada Prasanna Mohanty. 2016i. Kathaa Module Group : Sampark Hindi Urdu Translation Pipeline Modules. https://github.com/kathaa/hindi-urdu-modules. [Online; accessed 16-October-2016].

Brad A. Myers. 1990. Taxonomies of visual programming and program visualization. *J. Vis. Lang. Comput.*, 1(1):97–123.

2016. Sampark: Machine translation among indian languages. http://sampark.iiit.ac.in/sampark/web/index.php/content. Accessed: 2016-02-10.

Rajeev Sangal and Dipti Misra Sharma. 2001. Creating language resources for nlp in indian languages 1. background.

Nan C Shu. 1988. *Visual programming*. Van Nostrand Reinhold.

Stefan Tilkov and Steve Vinoski. 2010. Node. js: Using javascript to build high-performance network programs. *IEEE Internet Computing*, 14(6):80.

The LAPPS Grid: Current State and Next Steps

Nancy Ide, Keith Suderman
Department of Computer Science
Vassar College
Poughkeepsie, New York USA
`{ide,suderman}@cs.vassar.edu`

Eric Nyberg
Language Technology Institute
Carnegie Mellon University
Pittsburgh, Pennsylvania USA
`ehn@cs.cmu.edu`

James Pustejovsky, Marc Verhagen
Department of Computer Science
Brandeis University
Waltham, Massachusetts USA
`{jamesp,marc}@cs.brandeis.edu`

Abstract

The US National Science Foundation (NSF) SI^2-funded LAPPS Grid project has developed an open-source platform for enabling complex analyses while hiding complexities associated with underlying infrastructure, that can be accessed through a web interface, deployed on any Unix system, or run from the cloud. It provides sophisticated tool integration and history capabilities, a workflow system for building automated multi-step analyses, state-of-the-art evaluation capabilities, and facilities for sharing and publishing analyses. This paper describes the current facilities available in the LAPPS Grid and outlines the project's ongoing activities to enhance the framework.

1 Introduction

The US National Science Foundation (NSF) SI^2-funded LAPPS Grid project is a collaborative effort among Vassar College, Brandeis University, Carnegie-Mellon University (CMU), and the Linguistic Data Consortium (LDC) at the University of Pennsylvania. The LAPPS Grid is an open-source platform for enabling complex analyses while hiding complexities associated with underlying infrastructure. The platform can be accessed through a web interface, deployed on any Unix system, or run from the cloud. It provides sophisticated tool integration and history capabilities, a workflow system for building automated multi-step analyses, state-of-the-art evaluation capabilities, and facilities for sharing and publishing analyses. The LAPPS Grid is highly customizable and integrates with a wide variety of computing environments, ranging from laptop computers to clusters to compute clouds. The LAPPS Grid is part of the Federated Grid of Language Services (FGLS) (Ishida et al., 2014), a multi-lingual, international network of web service grids and providers in Asia and Europe, and is currently federating with two major frameworks in the pan-European CLARIN project. Through these federations, LAPPS Grid users have interoperable access to all the tools and modules in the other platforms, thus creating the largest network of interoperable components for language-related analysis and activity in the world.

This paper describes the current facilities available in the LAPPS Grid, which have been continually expanded over the past year, and provides an overview of the ways in which the LAPPS Grid compares to similar frameworks. We also outline the project's ongoing activities to enhance the framework, in particular its collaboration with the developers of the Galaxy framework and creation of educational materials.

Proceedings of WLSI/OIAF4HLT,
pages 11–18, Osaka, Japan, December 12 2016.

2 Current facilities

The LAPPS Grid currently provides a broad suite of interoperable Human Language Technologies (HLT) tools and data, and provides facilities for service discovery, service composition (including automatic format conversion between tools where necessary), performance evaluation (via provision of component-level measures for standard evaluation metrics for component-level and end-to-end measurement), and resource delivery for a range of language resources, including holdings of the Linguistic Data Consortium (LDC).[1] The list of HLT processing tools and resources currently available in the LAPPS Grid can be found at http://www.lappsgrid.org/language-services and includes dozens of the most commonly used HLT toolkits. In addition, through our federation with international partners, LAPPS Grid users have (or will soon have) access to hundreds of multi-lingual and multi-modal tools, applications, evaluation tools, lexicons, and data sources[2].

The key feature of the LAPPS Grid that differentiates it from most other platforms is the *interoperability* among tools and services, which is achieved through adoption of standard protocols and formats together with the development of additional standards for interchange. Syntactic interoperability among LAPPS Grid services is ensured by a JSON-LD format called the LAPPS Interchange Format (LIF) that groups annotations in views, where each view contains metadata that spells out the information contained in that view, including information necessary to determine compatibility with other tools and data. Semantic interoperability is achieved via references to definitions in the Web Services Exchange Vocabulary (WSEV). The WSEV has been built bottom up, driven by the needs of components in the LAPPS Grid and closely following standard practice in the field as well as adopting, where possible, existing terminology and type systems. Both LIF and the WSEV are described in detail elsewhere (Verhagen et al., 2016; Ide et al., 2014; Ide et al., 2016).

Another distinctive feature of the LAPPS Grid is its Open Advancement (OA) Evaluation system, a sophisticated environment that was used to develop IBM's Jeopardy-winning Watson. OA can be simultaneously applied to multiple variant workflows involving alternative tools for a given task, and the results are evaluated and displayed so that the best possible configuration is readily apparent. Similarly, the weak links in a chain are easily detected, which can lead to module-specific improvements that affect the entire process. The inputs, tools, parameters and settings used for each step in an analysis are recorded, thereby ensuring that each result can be exactly reproduced and reviewed later, and any tool configuration can be repeatedly applied to different data.

Several HLT software developers and projects have contributed their components and systems for inclusion in the LAPPS Grid, in order to provide exposure of these tools to a wide user audience and, crucially, to render them interoperable with other tools in the LAPPS Grid, thus allowing for their immediate inclusion in workflows supporting sophisticated applications as well as evaluation of their performance side-by-side with comparable components. Although many contributors host their own contributed services (which are called from within the LAPPS Grid), where necessary the LAPPS Grid provides hosting to ensure that software remains available to the community. Recently contributed tools include all core tools from University of Darmstadt's DKPro[3], the AIFdb services for Argumentation analysis[4] (Lawrence et al., 2012), the SWIFT Aligner for cross-lingual transfer (Gilmanov et al., 2014), the EDISON feature extraction framework[5] (Sammons et al., 2016) and other tools available from the University of Illinois (e.g., semantic role labelers, entity extractors), among others. In addition, several of the basic components produced by the ARIEL team working within DARPA's Low Resource Languages for Emergent Incidents (LORELEI) program have been integrated into the LAPPS Grid, which include tools and data to support a wide array of under-resourced languages.

The LAPPS Grid has been adopted by a Mellon-funded project at the University of Illinois, which is utilizing the platform to apply sophisticated HLT text mining methods to the HathiTrust Research

---

[1] http://www.ldc.upenn.edu

[2] For example, see http://langrid.org/service_manager/language-services for a partial list of services available though the FGLS, and https://vlo.clarin.eu/ for tools and resources available through CLARIN.

[3] https://dkpro.github.io

[4] http://www.aifdb.org

[5] https://cogcomp.cs.illinois.edu/page/software_view/Edison

Center's (HTRC) massive digital library)[6], in order enhance search and discovery across the library by complementing traditional volume-level bibliographic metadata with new metadata, using specially-developed LAPPS Grid-based CL applications. Finally, we are currently working with IBM to integrate its Watson services into the LAPPS Grid so that they will be available for community use for the first time, and interoperate with the very wide range of HLT modules the LAPPS Grid provides. This will open the door to rapid evaluation of alternative component pipelines using state-of-the-art metrics and procedures.

The LAPPS Grid uses Docker[7], a recently developed and increasingly popular virtualization platform, as a way to distribute and deploy the complete LAPPS Grid or parts thereof. Docker images are completely self-contained: users can download docker images and run them on their own servers or laptops or in the cloud without the need to install supporting components. We currently have several docker virtual servers running versions of the LAPPS Grid on Amazon Web Services and JetStream (http://jetstream-cloud.org).

To provide an intuitive, easy-to-use interface and management system, the LAPPS Grid project adopted the Galaxy framework (Giardine et al., 2005), a robust, well-developed platform that includes tool integration and history capabilities. together with a workflow system for building automated multi-step analyses, a visualization framework including visual analysis capabilities, and facilities for sharing and publishing analyses (Goecks et al., 2012). In addition to providing an intuitive user interface for workflow composition appropriate for non-technical users, Galaxy also provides support for replication of experiments and sharing of methods and results via automatic recording of all inputs, tools, parameters and settings in an experiment and provisions for sharing datasets, histories, and workflows via web links.[8] Replication capabilities are a vital need in the field of HLT, which has been plagued by a chronic lack of potential for replicability and reuse described in several recent publications (Pedersen, 2008; Fokkens et al., 2013), blogs[9], and workshops[10]. Facilities for reproducibility also enable users to develop organized catalogs of reusable workflows, rather than starting from scratch each time or trying to navigate a collection of *ad hoc* analysis scripts, and/or apply a command history to different data.

We have contributed Galaxy wrappers to call all LAPPS Grid web services to the Galaxy ToolShed[11]. The enables user to create a LAPPS/Galaxy instance locally or in the cloud that includes only the Galaxy "NLP Flavor" (in Galaxy terminology), which comprises all and only LAPPS Grid services and resources, if so desired.

The LAPPS Grid benefits from the Galaxy team's integration of interactive analysis environments, including Jupyter (Perez and Granger, 2007) and RStudio (Gandrud, 2013). Jupyter in particular is of interest to LAPPS Grid users; the LAPPS Grid team has developed a LAPPS Grid Services DSL[12] (LSD) kernel that can be used to interact with the LAPPS Grid services.[13] Jupyter Notebooks can contain executable code and documentation in one location, thus allowing fast templating and prototyping of services. There is no need to compile Java/Groovy code and deploy services to web servers for evaluation and testing, thus making it easy for students and non-technical users to develop sophisticated workflows and/or add their own components with no programming effort. Jupyter also provides "human in the loop" functionality, by allowing one to run a pipeline in the LAPPS Grid, manipulate the Galaxy history items in Jupyter, and finally upload the results to Galaxy for further processing. This facility is especially important for HLT development that involves iterative enhancement of training data on the basis of error analysis, etc.

---

[6] https://www.hathitrust.org

[7] https://www.docker.com/

[8] See (Goecks et al., 2010) for a comprehensive overview of Galaxy's sharing and publication capabilities.

[9] E.g., http://nlpers.blogspot.com/2006/11/reproducible-results.html

[10] E.g., Replicability and Reusability in Natural Language Processing: from Data to Software Sharing: http://nl.ijs.si/rrnlp2015/

[11] https://toolshed.g2.bx.psu.edu

[12] Groovy Domain Specific Language.

[13] The kernel is available from https://github.com/lappsgrid-incubator/jupyter-lsd-kernel; see also http://wiki.lappsgrid.org/technical/jupyter.html. A Docker image is also available including Jupyter and the LSD kernel, for installation-free usage.

3   Comparison with other frameworks

The LAPPS Grid differs from existing frameworks primarily because of the standards for interoperability it implements to enable components from different sources to be seamlessly interfaced, and the resulting ease and transparency with which components can be added and manipulated. Frameworks such as UIMA and GATE, which also provide multiple tools that can be pipelined together, require a relatively steep learning curve to use and considerable programming effort to add or modify components. Similarly, the Natural Language Toolkit (NLTK) requires Python programming and effectively limits the user to the tools that are built-in to the system. In contrast, modules can be easily added to the LAPPS Grid by wrapping them as a service, using provided templates; and, more importantly, no programming experience or technical expertise is required, since workflows are constructed using the Galaxy project's workflow management framework. This makes the LAPPS Grid ideal for instructional use.

The recently introduced Kathaa system (Mohanty et al., 2016) provides functionality similar to the LAPPS Grid, but allows modules to be interfaced only if compatible with one another–i.e., there is no attempt to standardize inputs and outputs among modules, so that mixing and matching of different tools that perform the same function is limited. The LAPPS Grid's Open Advancement evaluation modules, which exploit the ability to construct alternative pipelines in order produce statistics identifying the most effective tool sequence and/or components accounting for the largest proportion of error, are also unique; Kathaa in contrast has only basic evaluation facilities.

Another similar framework is the Alveo system (Cassidy et al., 2014), which also uses Galaxy as its workflow engine and renders tools interoperable using representations that are the same as, or isomorphic to, the LAPPS Grid's. Alveo is dedicated primarily to multi-modal data and applications and therefore includes a very different suite of modules and datasets; in the future, federating with Alveo could enable access to its facilities from within the LAPPS Grid.

4   Collaboration with Galaxy

Since the LAPPS Grid project adopted Galaxy in late 2014, we have had multiple interactions with the Galaxy development team to extend and/or modify Galaxy to meet some of our needs. These interactions have been so successful and mutually beneficial that our two projects are establishing a collaboration that will contribute to the continued development of both infrastructures. We believe that the synergistic development of capabilities supporting both HLT and genomic analysis within the Galaxy framework could have a significant impact on both fields, not only by enhancing Galaxy functionality overall, but also by integrating data, tools, as well as workflows and methods from previously distinct scientific communities. For example, HLT researchers will benefit from access to sophisticated visualization software for display and analysis of results common to research in the life sciences, but rarely used in HLT research, and biologists will be able to take advantage of bio-oriented HLT web services for mining of bio-entities and relations from textual sources and (via capabilities already present in Galaxy) integrate them into existing bio-data resources and analysis tools.

There are several key enhancements to Galaxy that are necessary to scale the LAPPS Grid to handle sophisticated HLT development and education that are synergistic with enhancements that the Galaxy team is already proposing to benefit life sciences research. These include the ability to efficiently handle large data collections (i.e., a large number of small datasets, vs. the single large dataset common in genomics research); and enhanced ability to investigate data using Interactive Environments (IEs), which is intended to assist life sciences research by allowing for injection of visual analytics in a workflow, but for HLT would provide "human-in-the-loop" capabilities to support iterative improvement in machine learning. At the same time, the Galaxy developers have proposed enhancements to their framework that are already in development for LAPPS Grid tools, for example, automatic management of software dependencies (both syntactic and semantic), and systematic workflow exploration and optimization, as provided in our OA evaluation suite of tools. Thus the collaboration can provide significant benefits to both the HLT and life sciences communities.

The two projects are also working together to create automatic workflow creation capabilities, such as a "Pipeline Wizard" to provide a wizard-like interface to guide the user through the logical steps in creating instances of known workflow(s); and/or a "Pipeline-via-Dialog" that allows the user to specify the desired analytic goal in simple English, where the system constructs the desired workflow automatically.

The LAPPS Grid will also benefit from Galaxy's efforts to expand their access to the Extreme Science and Engineering Discovery Environment (XSEDE) (Towns et al., 2014) and JetStream, to which the LAPPS Grid has recently deployed several cloud-based instances for use in courses and specific projects. The Galaxy team is implementing means to take full advantage of High Performance Computing resources, including parallelization and scaling support, as well as the latest dependency management, code versioning, and virtualization techniques, all of which will serve LAPPS Grid needs. Our collaboration will ensure that implementation within Galaxy of these and other capabilities that can serve both disciplines are flexible and scalable to other disciplines' needs in the future. It will also enable gathering user feedback from the perspectives of both communities to feed development of both platforms.

4.1 Federation with CLARIN

The Mellon Foundation recently funded a collaborative effort make the LAPPS Grid interoperable with the pan-European CLARIN project's WebLicht/Tübingen[14] and LINDAT/CLARIN (Prague)[15] frameworks. The effort will create a "trust network" among the LAPPS Grid and CLARIN sites, in order to to make the services we currently provide, as well as future services we will develop, transparently interoperable and mutually accessible from our respective infrastructures. A focus of activity will be to adapt the LAPPS Grid to accommodate the Shibboleth (SAML 2) protocol in order to allow access to login-protected (but otherwise generally accessible) content and services by anyone authenticated through the CLARIN authentication and identification mechanism.

Collaborative access between the LAPPS Grid and CLARIN is achievable largely due to standards and best practices for interoperability that have emerged over the past decade and that were applied internally to both the LAPPS Grid and CLARIN. The federation with CLARIN complements the LAPPS Grid's membership in the Federated Grid of Language Services (FGLS), which provides interoperable access to the University of Kyoto's Language Grid[16] and four other Asian grids, plus a grid under development at the European Language Resources Association (ELRA)[17]. Through these two federations we have vastly increased the availability of multi-lingual and multi-modal resources and tools in the LAPPS Grid and expanded the range of users beyond the HLT community we originally intended to serve, including users involved in inter-cultural communication and the digital humanities research.

4.2 Course development

The LAPPS Grid team recently developed and delivered a four-day short course on Intelligent Information Systems for Analysts, using a purpose-built instance of the LAPPS Grid software deployed in the cloud. The LAPPS Grid "Discovery" instance supports access to selected corpora from the LDC Gigaword data source, along with a variety of open-source HLT tools (sentence splitters, named entity recognizers, passage extractors, passage rankers), and was the focus of hands-on exercises for comparative evaluation of HLT components, composition of analytic pipelines from individual components, and analytic approaches that can learn from user knowledge and feedback.

Based on this experience, we recognized that the LAPPS Grid is an ideal framework to help students interact with and design complex HLT systems without the need for sophisticated technical skills. To that end, we are focusing on the development of curriculum materials to enable students to learn the skills required to rapidly analyze large bodies of language data in practical contexts, in collaboration with several partners at universities in the US, Canada, and Europe (Brandeis University, Carnegie Mellon University, Vassar College, University of Dundee (Scotland), George Washington University, and University of British Columbia). The course materials are being designed to effectively teach to a first-year computer science or computational linguistics student the skills required to create new analytic modules, compose pipelines integrating those modules, and compare them to pipelines which integrate existing services–all

---

[14]http://weblicht.sfs.uni-tuebingen.de/

[15]https://lindat.mff.cuni.cz/

[16]http://langrid.org

[17]http://www.elra.info.

without the often prohibitive need to acquire and manage data sets and software suites on an individual basis–within the context of on-line, self-driven, hands-on exercises supported by the LAPPS Grid.

A secondary goal is to effectively teach to a first-year computer science graduate student the skills required to compose, evaluate and optimize state-of-the-art software solutions using standard datasets, evaluation metrics and corpora for multi-language, multi-media information systems that process text, audio, images and video. Providing such a capability for graduate instruction would unlock the potential of the vast store of data present in repositories such as the Linguistic Data Consortium and the multi-lingual resources available from federated grids. The end result will be to train the next generation of HLT researchers, developers, and language analysts, who will use advanced technologies such as the LAPPS Grid on a regular basis to augment simpler analyses available via web search and the use of standalone tools.

All course materials will be freely available from the Open Learning Initiative (OLI)[18] and a dedicated repository maintained by the LAPPS Grid project. The materials will be accompanied with ready-made docker images that can be used as is or easily customized to suit specific pedagogical goals.

5 Enhancement of Open Advancement Evaluation Capabilities

A final focus of current activity is extension of the component and pipeline evaluation capabilities in the LAPPS Grid to support parallel evaluation and broader adoption by end-user communities. These include

- parallel exploration of alternative pipelines, drawing on recent work on Configuration Space Exploration (CSE) and Phased Ranking Models (Garduno et al., 2013; Yang et al., 2013; Liu and Nyberg, 2013). We will provide the capability to specify an abstract pipeline with multiple possible components per phase, and the corresponding capability to explore the different alternatives automatically in parallel using the CSE technique.

- accessible display of results, with support for different visualizations for pipeline results (both the data objects produced by the pipeline as well as the evaluation metrics measured for each pipeline test).

Our federation with multiple grids and frameworks will make it possible to evaluate the performance of vast arrays of alternative tool pipelines that would otherwise be unavailable or prohibitively difficult to use together. It will also provide, for the first time, the capability to study and evaluate tools performance on data in a huge set of different languages.

6 Future Developments and Conclusion

The LAPPS Grid project is developing in two main directions. First, it is expanding not only the range of tools, resources, and components available within the framework itself, but also providing access to hundreds, if not thousands, of resources and tools available from federated partners. Second, it is focusing on development of cloud-deployed, customizable course materials that can dramatically enhance the training of the next generation of HLT researchers, and provide significantly improved materials for non-technical users.

In addition to the above developments, we are also engaging in significant community outreach to encourage tool developers to contribute to the LAPPS Grid repository, through which process they become interoperable with all other the LAPPS Grid tools and components. Ultimately, by this means and federation with other grids and frameworks throughout the world, we hope to develop a massive library of interoperable components for HLT research, development, and education.

Acknowledgements

The work described here is supported by US National Science Foundation awards ACI-1147912, ACI-1147944, ACI-1547621, and ACI-1547270, and a grant from the Mellon Foundation.

---

[18]http://oli.cmu.edu

References

Steve Cassidy, Dominique Estival, Timothy Jones, Denis Burnham, and Jared Burghold. 2014. The Alveo Virtual Laboratory: A Web based Repository API. In *Proceedings of the Ninth International Conference on Language Resources and Evaluation (LREC'14)*, Reykjavik, Iceland, may. European Language Resources Association (ELRA).

Antske Fokkens, Marieke van Erp, Marten Postma, Ted Pedersen, Piek Vossen, and Nuno Freire. 2013. Offspring from Reproduction Problems: What Replication Failure Teaches Us. In *Proceedings of the Conference of The Association for Computational Linguistics*, pages 1691–1701. The Association for Computational Linguistics.

C. Gandrud. 2013. *Reproducible Research with R and RStudio*. CRC Press.

Elmer Garduno, Zi Yang, Avner Maiberg, Collin McCormack, Yan Fang, and Eric Nyberg. 2013. CSE Framework: A UIMA-based Distributed System for Configuration Space Exploration Unstructured Information Management Architecture. In Peter Klgl, Richard Eckart de Castilho, and Katrin Tomanek, editors, *UIMA@GSCL*, CEUR Workshop Proceedings, pages 14–17. CEUR-WS.org.

B. Giardine, C. Riemer, R. C. Hardison, R. Burhans, L. Elnitski, P. Shah, Y. Zhang, D. Blankenberg, I. Albert, J. Taylor, W. Miller, W. J. Kent, and A. Nekrutenko. 2005. Galaxy: a platform for interactive large-scale genome analysis. *Genome Research*, 15(10):1451–55.

Timur Gilmanov, Olga Scrivner, and Sandra Kbler. 2014. SWIFT Aligner, A Multifunctional Tool for Parallel Corpora: Visualization, Word Alignment, and (Morpho)-Syntactic Cross-Language Transfer. In *Proceedings of the Ninth International Conference on Language Resources and Evaluation (LREC'14)*, Reykjavik, Iceland, may. European Language Resources Association (ELRA).

Jeremy Goecks, Anton Nekrutenko, and James Taylor. 2010. Galaxy: a comprehensive approach for supporting accessible, reproducible, and transparent computational research in the life sciences. *Genome biology*, 11:R86.

Jeremy Goecks, Nate Coraor, The Galaxy Team, Anton Nekrutenko, and James Taylor. 2012. NGS Analyses by Visualization with Trackster. *Nature Biotechnology*, 30(11):10361039.

Nancy Ide, James Pustejovsky, Keith Suderman, and Marc Verhagen. 2014. The Language Application Grid Web Service Exchange Vocabulary. In *Proceedings of the Workshop on Open Infrastructures and Analysis Frameworks for HLT (OIAF4HLT)*, Dublin, Ireland.

Nancy Ide, Keith Suderman, Marc Verhagen, and James Pustejovsky. 2016. The Language Application Grid Web Service Exchange Vocabulary. In *Revised Selected Papers of the Second International Workshop on Worldwide Language Service Infrastructure - Volume 9442*, WLSI 2015, pages 18–32, New York, NY, USA. Springer-Verlag New York, Inc.

Toru Ishida, Yohei Murakami, Donghui Lin, Takao Nakaguchi, and Masayuki Otani. 2014. Open Language Grid–Towards a Global Language Service Infrastructure. In *The Third ASE International Conference on Social Informatics (SocialInformatics 2014)*, Cambridge, Massachusetts, USA.

John Lawrence, Floris Bex, Chris Reed, and Mark Snaith. 2012. AIFdb: Infrastructure for the Argument Web. In *Computational Models of Argument - Proceedings of COMMA 2012, Vienna, Austria, September 10-12, 2012*, pages 515–516.

Rui Liu and Eric Nyberg. 2013. A Phased Ranking Model for Question Answering. In *Proceedings of the CIKM'13*.

Sharada Prasanna Mohanty, Nehal J Wani, Manish Srivastava, and Dipti Misra Sharma. 2016. Kathaa: A visual programming framework for nlp applications. In *Proceedings of the 2016 Conference of the North American Chapter of the Association for Computational Linguistics: Demonstrations*, pages 92–96, San Diego, California, June. Association for Computational Linguistics.

Ted Pedersen. 2008. Empiricism is Not a Matter of Faith. *Computational Linguistics*, 34(3), September.

Fernando Perez and Brian E. Granger. 2007. IPython: A System for Interactive Scientific Computing. *Computing in Science and Engg.*, 9(3):21–29, May.

Mark Sammons, Christos Christodoulopoulos, Parisa Kordjamshidi, Daniel Khashabi, Vivek Srikumar, Paul Vijayakumar, Mazin Bokhari, Xinbo Wu, and Dan Roth. 2016. EDISON: Feature Extraction for NLP, Simplified. In *Proceedings of the Tenth International Conference on Language Resources and Evaluation (LREC 2016)*. European Language Resources Association (ELRA).

John Towns, Timothy Cockerill, Maytal Dahan, Ian T. Foster, Kelly P. Gaither, Andrew S. Grimshaw, Victor Hazlewood, Scott Lathrop, David Lifka, Gregory D. Peterson, Ralph Roskies, J. Ray Scott, and Nancy Wilkins-Diehr. 2014. XSEDE: Accelerating Scientific Discovery. *Computing in Science and Engineering*, 16(5):62–74.

Marc Verhagen, Keith Suderman, Di Wang, Nancy Ide, Chunqi Shi, Jonathan Wright, and James Pustejovsky. 2016. The LAPPS Interchange Format. In *Revised Selected Papers of the Second International Workshop on Worldwide Language Service Infrastructure - Volume 9442*, WLSI 2015, pages 33–47, New York, NY, USA. Springer-Verlag New York, Inc.

Zi Yang, Elmer Garduno, Yan Fang, Avner Maiberg, Collin McCormack, and Eric Nyberg. 2013. Building Optimal Information Systems Automatically: Configuration Space Exploration for Biomedical Information Systems. In *Proceedings of the CIKM'13*.

Automatic Analysis of Flaws in Pre-Trained NLP Models

Richard Eckart de Castilho
Ubiquitous Knowledge Processing Lab (UKP-TUDA)
Department of Computer Science
Technische Universität Darmstadt
`http://www.ukp.tu-darmstadt.de/`

Abstract

Most tools for natural language processing (NLP) today are based on machine learning and come with pre-trained models. In addition, third-parties provide pre-trained models for popular NLP tools. The predictive power and accuracy of these tools depends on the quality of these models. Downstream researchers often base their results on pre-trained models instead of training their own. Consequently, pre-trained models are an essential resource to our community. However, to be best of our knowledge, no systematic study of pre-trained models has been conducted so far. This paper reports on the analysis of 274 pre-models for six NLP tools and four potential causes of problems: *encoding*, *tokenization*, *normalization*, and *change* over time. The analysis is implemented in the open source tool *Model Investigator*. Our work 1) allows model consumers to better assess whether a model is suitable for their task, 2) enables tool and model creators to sanity-check their models before distributing them, and 3) enables improvements in tool inter-operability by performing automatic adjustments of normalization or other pre-processing based on the models used.

1 Introduction

As natural language processing (NLP) has become a pervasive technology in many research and application domains, NLP tools and the pre-trained models that ship with them or that are provided by third parties have become essential resources. Often, researchers and other users do not have access to text corpora from which they could train suitable models themselves or simply prefer the convenience of using existing models. Users of centrally provided NLP infrastructures may not even have the option of using models other that those offered within the platform. However, this entails that any problems with these models, propagate into subsequent NLP components in a pipeline or into data analytics and negatively influence them. Worst of all, the consumers of pre-trained models may not even be aware of the problems the models exhibit.

We hope to raise more awareness through this paper by reporting on an analysis of pre-trained models for typical sources of problems: *encoding*, *tokenization*, *normalization*, and *changes* between different released versions (Section 3). The analysis is based on a dataset of 274 pre-trained models for six popular NLP tools. To the best of our knowledge, this is the first systematic analysis of pre-trained models for flaws and other sources of problems. We have observed that some models have been distributed with serious flaws for years and have informed the model creators of the problems.

The open source tool *Model Investigator*[1] that was created and used to perform this analysis (Section 2). It can be used by model creators to perform automatic sanity checks on their models and by model consumers to obtain detailed information about new models as they become available. The modular tool can easily be extended to support pre-trained models of new NLP tools.

Finally, we investigate the negative impact of flawed models in a case study: models trained with a bad character encoding (Section 4).

---

[1] `https://github.com/UKPLab/coling2016-modelinspector`

Proceedings of WLSI/OIAF4HLT,
pages 19–27, Osaka, Japan, December 12 2016.

1.1 The role of models in NLP pipelines

Before going into the details, we briefly motivate why the analyzed issues are typical sources of problems in NLP pipelines, in particular when mixing components and models from different vendors.

Combining multiple NLP tools into pipelines is a typical task that is hindered by the fact that the tools tend to come with different APIs and input/output formats. There is a range of frameworks and platforms such as UIMA (Ferrucci and Lally, 2004), GATE (Cunningham et al., 2011), WebLicht (Hinrichs et al., 2010), LAP (Lapponi et al., 2013), DKPro Core (Eckart de Castilho and Gurevych, 2014) and LAPPS Grid (Ide et al., 2014) that address this problem by each respectively providing common data exchange models between NLP tools. Tool wrappers ensure that the data is transformed between the common exchange model and the tool-specific input/output formats, e.g. between the UIMA CAS exchange model and the input/output format used by the Stanford Parser. This process of wrapping NLP tools coming from entirely different contexts requires paying close attention to all kinds of variations in data representation, tagsets being used, etc. This requires not at last having detailed information about models and their characteristics.

A tool wrapper needs to know how to transform the data, e.g. which kinds normalization to apply to the text before passing it on to the tool, which character encoding to use, etc. This information can be hard-coded into the wrapper, but this is inflexible. It can be provided via parameters that a user needs to supply, but this is error prone. It could also be automatically obtained directly from the model file the tool is configured to use, but models are typically treated as black boxes. Extracting the necessary information is often not possible via the standard API. In many cases, we had to use invasive methods to extract e.g. lexicon information directly from *private variables*[2] in the model data objects.

Also, the interaction between components in a pipeline can have an impact. For example tokenization is typically the initial step in a pipeline and the resulting tokens are used by the other components. If the pipeline tokenization scheme does not correspond to the one that was used when a model was created, a negative impact on the pipeline results can be expected.

Some NLP tools have been around for many years and have seen multiple updates to their code and to their models. The models may have changed in significant, yet typically undocumented ways, e.g. with respect to normalization or lexicon size, which can have an impact on existing pipelines being upgraded to newer model versions. One might expect that there have been improvements that would produce better results when upgrading an old experimental setup to using a newer version of a tool or model. A positive change could be that newer models have been trained on more data and offer a larger vocabulary coverage. However, changes may also easily lead to decreased performance, e.g. if the normalization steps used when creating the model were changed and the pipeline setup is not adjusted accordingly.

2 The *Model Investigator* tool

To perform our analysis, we have implemented the open-source software *Model Investigator*. For the analysis, *Model Investigator* relies on extracting the lexicon information encoded in the models, i.e. the tokens the model was trained on. The lexicon is not always explicitly represented in a model. In some cases, it has to be extracted from different types of features representations according to the machine learning approach used by the respective tool.

Model Investigator can be used either as a command line tool or as a software library. Its architecture consists of three main component types: *model analyzers*, *checks*, and *reports*.

Model Analyzers A model analyzer extracts the lexicon information from a given model file. To support a new NLP tool, a new model analyzer needs to be implemented. The method of extracting the lexicon is specific for each tool. While some models contain an explicit lexicon, for others it needs to be extracted from an inventory of feature names that are used by the machine learning part of the tool.

Typically, the model analyzer loads a model into memory using the deserialization provided by the respective tool. As most of the analyzed tools have been implemented for the Java Virtual Machine (JVM),

---

[2]Many programming languages allow to control the visibility of data and functionality. The *private* functions and variables are meant not to be used by third parties, usually because they may be subject to change between different version of a software package without further notice. Without special effort, such functions and variables cannot be accessed.

we used the JVM-based language Groovy to implement our tool. Groovy has the benefit being able to ignore the typical Java access-modifiers (*private, protected*) and greatly facilitates accessing the often access-restricted data structures containing the lexicon information. Through integration with the Maven Central software repository, we could make it easy to automatically test a given model against different versions of a NLP tool, e.g. to test with which versions of the Stanford Parser and CoreNLP packages a given model is compatible. This way, we could inspect the models of all of the analyzed tools except TreeTagger, which is not implemented in Java. To analyze the TreeTagger models, we had to reverse-engineer the undocumented format of the binary model files to extract the lexicon information.

Checks   The checks are then used to test the extracted lexicon for potential problems. A range of checks related to *encoding, tokenization*, and *normalization* have been implemented (cf. Sections 3.1-3.3). New checks can be added easily. The checks performed by the tool fall into two categories: *boolean checks* (e.g. if escaped and non-escaped brackets appear at the same time) and *frequency checks* (e.g. how many lexicon words contain encoding problems). As most of the models contain a small number of problems, we report only those frequency check results that affect more than 1% of the lexicon entries. Not all models are versioned and not all models change across releases of a tool. Thus, as the model version we use the date of the first change detected by calculating and comparing a checksum over the different model files in a series. If exactly the same model is contained in multiple versions of a NLP software package, we count it only once.

Reports   The primary output of *Model Investigator* are detailed per-model analysis reports that are written as machine-processable JSON files. In addition, *Model Investigator* also generates comparative diachronic reports for models which are available in multiple versions. We leveraged this to analyze the ways in which models in a series *change* from one release to the next (cf. Section 3.4). Overview reports are generated as CSV files which can be opened using most spreadsheet applications.

3   Model Analysis

This section examines different types of issues related to encoding, tokenization, and normalization that were observed in the analyzed models. We exclude questions related to coverage because typically a frequency cutoff is applied during the training process and thus the lexicon extracted from a model usually does not give a complete account of the tokens in the training corpus.

As the basis for our analysis, we have compiled a dataset[3] of 274 pre-trained models for six NLP tools: POS tagger and named entity recognizer from Apache OpenNLP[4]; POS tagger, parser, and named entity recognizer from Stanford CoreNLP (Manning et al., 2014); TreeTagger (Schmid, 1994) (Table 1).

In order to track changes over time, we have organized the 274 models into *series*. Each series represents what should be considered as a set of different versions of essentially the same model. Such a series would e.g. cover the English PCFG models from the Stanford Parser that were included with different releases of the Stanford Parser package and the Stanford CoreNLP package. We have analyzed 48 series of size > 1.

3.1   Character Encoding

Problem description   Special care has to be taken when creating a model with respect to 1) the encoding of the corpora used as training data and 2) with respect to the default encoding used on the platform where the model is created. Older (western) corpora often use variations of the ISO 8859 encoding, whereas newer corpora tend to use a Unicode encoding, often UTF-8. As for the platforms that models are trained on: the default (western) encoding for Windows is ISO 8859; UTF-8 is commonly the default on Linux and OS X (depending on the version, also Mac OS Roman). This heterogeneity of encodings makes training a model an error-prone task that requires careful attention. We observe two typical problems related to encoding:

---

[3]Some TreeTagger models that were collected in the past are no longer publicly available from the TreeTagger homepage. Since the license of the TreeTagger models does not allow for redistribution, we can unfortunately not make them available.

[4]`http://opennlp.apache.org`

Tool ID	Product	Tool	Languages	Series	Models
C-TAG	CoreNLP	POS tagger	6	23	70
O-TAG	OpenNLP	POS tagger	8	22	22
T-TAG	TreeTagger	POS tagger	18	18	23
C-NER	CoreNLP	Named Entity Recognizer	3	15	33
O-NER	OpenNLP	Named Entity Recognizer	3	15	15
C-PAR	CoreNLP	Parser	6	25	111
Total			21	118	274

Table 1: Analyzed tools, series, and models

Type A) Non-UTF-8 data is read as UTF-8. Non-ASCII characters that are not valid in UTF-8 are replaced with the Unicode replacement character (U+FFFD). This is a destructive operation as the original character information is lost. There are variation of this problem that use other characters as a replacement, e.g. the question mark. We did not analyze these variations here.

Type B) UTF-8 is read as ISO 8859 and re-encoded into UTF-8. In this case, UTF-8 characters are treated as one or more ISO 8859 characters, depending on the number of bytes used to encode the character in UTF-8. E.g. "á" (UTF-8) becomes "Ã¡" (ISO 8859-1). This is a non-destructive operation as the ISO 8859 byte sequence can be recovered and then re-interpreted as UTF-8.

Implementation The checks for type A flaws count the numbers of entries in the model lexicon containing question marks and Unicode replacement characters respectively. The check for a type B flaw is more sophisticated. Here, a set of *seed characters* is generated from those characters which differ between the different ISO 8859 variants, i.e. non-ASCII characters in the code range from 0xA1 to 0xFF. These seed characters are converted from the source encoding to a UTF-8 sequence which is then again re-encoded using the source encoding. The check then counts the number of model lexicon entries containing these re-encoded seed characters.

Result We observe serious type A flaws in 5 models of 3 series. For type B flaws, we checked against ISO 8859-(1,2,5,6) and used only the results for the encoding with the most hits. 7 models of 4 series exhibit serious type B encoding problems likely due to misconfiguration during model training. In both cases, we report only analysis results on the latest model version exhibiting the problem in the respective series (Table 2), which is also the latest version available at the time of writing. Additionally, we list first version affected version in each series from our dataset. It can be seen that the flaws in the models exist for many years and have even be carried over to newer versions. A small number (2-50) of type A and B errors was observed in 12 additional models and are likely spurious mistakes in the underlying corpora.

The problems listed in Table 2 have been reported to the respective model creators. Some have acknowledged the problems and started looking into providing new fixed models.

Tool ID	Lang	Model	First affected version	Most recent version	Type	Affected lexicon entries* Rel.	Abs.
C-NER	de	hgc	20120522	20150130	A	16.37 %	2616
C-NER	de	dewac	20120522	20150130	A	16.47 %	2800
C-PAR	es	pcfg	20140826	20150108	B	18.82 %	6492
C-PAR	es	sr	20140828	20141023	B	19.76 %	4495
C-PAR	es	sr-beam	20140828	20141023	B	19.51 %	5654
O-TAG	de	maxent	20120616	20120616	B	16.70 %	2442

Table 2: Models with encoding problems (* affected entires for most recent version).

Recommendation   Developers of NLP tools should allow configuring the encoding independent of the platform a model is created on. Model creators must pay attention to configure the tools for the proper encoding of the source data. *Model Investigator* can be used to verify the encoding of the trained model.

3.2   Tokenization

Problem description   Tokenization is typically the first step in an NLP pipeline and most subsequent steps build on the generated units. This is true when training models, but also when applying them. Thus, it is important that the same tokenization scheme is used at both stages. However, models are often trained on manually segmented corpora which may be hard to reproduce automatically (cf. (Dridan and Oepen, 2012)). Another common case is that the model creator did not document the tokenization scheme and the unaware model consumer chooses to uses a different one. This leads to the question whether information about this scheme can be extracted from a model and can be used to advise the model consumer whether a particular given automatic segmentation tool is suitable in combination with this model. As a subsequent step, the model consumer may be informed whether different models used in a pipeline use similar or radically different segmentation schemes.

Implementation   As a heuristic for the suitability of a tokenizer for a given model, we apply the tokenizer to each lexicon word in turn and count cases in which the tokenizer further splits the lexicon word. For instance, if the lexicon word is [*1-million-plus*] and a given tokenizer splits it into [*1*, -, *million*, -, *plus*], this is counted. In addition to tokenizers from already introduced tools, we used the Java BreakIterator, JTok,[5] LanguageTool,[6] and LingPipe.[7] Due to the modular structure of *Model Investigator*, support for additional tokenizers can be easily added.

Result   Exemplary results for all English models (max. over all versions/series) are shown in Table 3. A high result should indicate that a tokenizer is *not* suitable. However, further interpretation of the results is difficult. Obviously the heuristic has two major problems: 1) a trivial tokenizer that does nothing at all produces optimal results; 2) most tokenizers are context sensitive but in our test each lexicon entry is analyzed individually without context. Further in-depth analysis correlating results to different token shapes (e.g. numbers, dates, chemical compounds, etc.) may yield additional insight as to whether a user should be concerned about a high split rate or not.

Tokenizer	O-NER	O-TAG	C-NER	C-PAR	C-TAG	T-TAG
Java BreakIterator	0.05	4.94	5.17	7.72	61.32	0.24
JTok	0.03	2.88	1.14	1.44	49.68	0.08
LanguageTool	0.05	7.71	8.37	10.66	14.72	0.26
LingPipe	0.01	15.55	10.34	18.77	64.08	10.44
OpenNLP	0.02	0.74	1.13	0.77	17.59	0.11
CoreNLP	0.02	3.00	0.99	2.06	3.43	0.15

Table 3: Percentage of split lexicon entries for English pre-trained models of six NLP tools

Recommendation   Model consumers should consider using *Model Investigator* to extract the lexicon from a pre-trained model and to apply their tokenizer of choice to it. If the tokenizers splits a significant number of the lexicon entries into smaller tokens, the tokenizer may not be suitable for use with the given model. Based on our analysis of pre-trained models and tokenizers, we conjecture a ratio of more than 20% split lexicon entries as unnecessarily high and potentially problematic.

3.3   Normalization

Problem description   Normalization is a common step while preparing corpora and training models on them. The most common and prominent normalization may be the that of brackets and quotes introduced

---

[5]http://github.com/DFKI-MLT/JTok
[6]http://languagetool.org
[7]http://alias-i.com/lingpipe

by the Penn Treebank (PTB) (Marcus et al., 1993) and used in many corpora thereafter. Here, e.g. a right round bracket " (" gets normalized to "-RRB-". But we also observe other kinds of normalization in the analyzed models, e.g. the escaping of slashes and underscores. Many models contain a small number of XML entities (1-5), but we did not find this to be a systematically applied step. CoreNLP includes a normalization step to *americanize* English text which we did not further analyze here.

In most cases, normalization can be easily detected from the model lexicon. However, to the best of our knowledge, no NLP tool or wrapper actually does inspect the user-provided model to automatically configure suitable normalization steps for the given model. Instead, it is assumed that the user knows which normalization is required and configures the pipeline accordingly. In particular, if different models for the same tool use different normalization schemes, the user may forget to adjust the settings accordingly when changing models.

If normalization is applied inconsistently during model training, it can negatively affect the results. For example, finding PTB-normalized and non-normalized brackets in a model lexicon may be a indicator of an inconsistently normalized corpus or of a bug in the normalization code.

A particular problem are *invisible* characters such as the non-breaking space (NBSP) and the zero-width soft hyphen (SHY). A visual scan of the corpus data does not reveal these. Normally, it cannot be assumed that such characters are used systematically in input data. For most users, models trained on corpora containing such characters will produce sub-optimal results.

Implementation The checks for normalization problems count the number of model lexicon entries containing particular substrings or characters, e.g. entries containing SHY, NPSP, escaped slashes, or PTB brackets and quotes respectively.

Result We analyzed the models looking for typical normalization steps (Table 4) and problem indicators (Table 5). Inconsistent normalization of brackets appears to be a problem in some models, mostly for CoreNLP NER. Mixed quotes are detected in a large number of models. We assume this to be an artifact of the tokenization scheme not splitting adjacent quotes into separate tokens rather than being a normalization problem. SHYs appear systematically in the Spanish CoreNLP models which were all trained on AnCora 3.0 (Taulé et al., 2008) and also in the Spanish OpenNLP NER models. The latter were trained on data from the Spanish EFE News Agency used in CoNLL-2002 which was later integrated into AnCora. NBSPs appear in a many models but not systematically.

Normalization		Series	Models
PTB curly brackets	-LCB-, -RCB-	27	82
PTB round brackets	-LRB-, -RRB-	20	119
PTB square brackets	-LSB-, -RSB-	10	26
PTB quotes	` ` , ' '	43	103
Slash escaped	\/	2	6

Table 4: Common normalizations

Issue	Series	Models	Max. affected lexicon entries
Mixed round brackets	7	10	-
Mixed square brackets	2	4	-
Mixed quotes	42	102	-
Contains SHY	7	10	4.40 %
Contains NBSP*	22	58	0.11 %

Table 5: Normalization issues (* no 1% cutoff)

Recommendation NBSPs should be replaced by regular a space character and SHYs should be removed from texts before training and analysis, actually even before tokenization. *Model Investigator* includes checks to test whether a trained model still contains problematic invisible characters in its lexicon and can be used to verify the final model.

3.4 Change between Model Versions

Problem description Some tools, such as CoreNLP and TreeTagger, are regularly updated or released in new versions. It is usually neither obvious nor documented if and in which way the models change as part of an update. Models packaged with different versions of a tool may actually be the same. For example the CoreNLP package has for a long time included a set of models with each released version of the package, but between two releases, only a few of these models changed. We also observe that models may change without any version number increasing. For example, the models available from the TreeTagger website are regularly updated, but their file name or version does not change in most cases. Users can only observe such changes if they download the models at different points in time and compare the binary files to each other bit-by-bit. If there *are* changes, they may have impact on the results. Negative impact could be caused e.g. by changes in the normalization. However, there could also be positive impact, e.g. if new models are trained on additional data and thus may provide additional coverage or accuracy.

Implementation To get an impression of the the change over time, we analyzed the oldest and the most recent model within each series and compared the results.

Results Of the 118 analyzed series, 48 consist of more than one model. Most of these remain largely stable in their lexicon size over time. Only 10 series exhibit a change of $> 1\%$ from the oldest to the newest model in the series (Table 6). This indicates that results based on most models should remain comparable irrespective of the model version used. On the other hand, it would have also been great to observe that training data is continually extended over the years.

Tool ID	Lang	Model	Affected lexicon entries oldest	newest	Δ Abs	Rel %
C-NER	en	all.3class.caseless.distsim.crf	32809	41092	8283	25.25
C-NER	en	all.3class.distsim.crf	24008	40572	16564	68.99
C-NER	en	conll.4class.distsim.crf	13677	13952	275	2.01
C-NER	en	muc.7class.distsim.crf	10364	10901	537	5.18
C-PAR	zh	factored	37687	55943	18256	48.44
C-PAR	zh	pcfg	37687	55943	18256	48.44
C-TAG	de	dewac	44581	47916	3335	7.48
C-TAG	de	fast	44581	47916	3335	7.48
C-TAG	de	hgc	44581	47916	3335	7.48
T-TAG	es	le	74289	84217	9928	13.36

Table 6: Series with lexicon size changes ($> 1\%$)

In terms of normalization, we find that some series switch from regular brackets to PTB brackets (round 4, square 5), from escaped slashes to unescaped slashes (2), and two series fix their issues of mixed PTB/normal brackets. It is also notable that in two cases (C-TAG *bidirectional-distsim*, *left3words-distsim*) the lexicon entries split by the JTok tokenizer drop by over 50% from 1666 to 800 due to a switch from escaped to unescaped slashes.

Recommendation Users should be careful when upgrading to a new version of a model and ensure that after the upgrade their setup still produces comparable results to before the upgrade. If the results change unexpectedly after the upgrade, *Model Investigator* can be used to get additional insight by generating a report of the characteristics of the old and new model and to comparing these to each other.

4 Case study: Impact of bad character encoding

In this section, we revisit the issue of models that were trained with a bad character encoding (cf. Section 3.1) and investigate the negative impact it has on the accuracy. We previously identified two series of models to be affected by a *type B* encoding problem: during the training of the model, an UTF-8 corpus was read as ISO 8859. Since this type of encoding problem is reversible, it is possible to transform the corpus tokens to the same broken encoding that is used in the model without any loss of information.

We measured the tagging accuracy of the German OpenNLP maxent POS tagger model once out-of-the-box and once transforming the tokens to the same broken encoding used in the model before passing them to the tagger. As evaluation datasets, we used the TIGER treebank (Brants et al., 2002) and on the TüBa D/Z treebank (Telljohann et al., 2004). Note that the German OpenNLP POS tagger model was originally trained on the TIGER corpus, so the accuracy on this corpus should not be taken as an indicator of the model quality, but only for the change in accuracy between broken and "fixed" encoding. The tagging accuracy of the model increases by 1.26 on the TüBa D/Z corpus and by 1.38 on the TIGER corpus when the tokens are transformed to the broken model encoding before passing them to the tagger.

In the same way, we tested the broken Spanish CoreNLP PCFG parser model. Note that we evaluated only the the POS tagging accuracy of the model, not the parsing accuracy. Due to a lack of any other Spanish corpus with a comparable tagset, again, we evaluated the model's accuracy against its training corpus. The model was trained on the AnCore 3.0.0 corpus. We evaluated against the 3.0.1 version of AnCora[8] and measured an improvement 5.05 in tagging accuracy when "fixing" the encoding.

Tool ID	Lang	Model	Version	Corpus	Encoding defect in	Accuracy		
						broken	fixed	Δ
O-TAG	de	maxent	20120616	TIGER 2.2	model	97.59	98.97	1.38
O-TAG	de	maxent	20120616	TüBa D/Z 10	model	92.66	93.92	1.26
C-PAR	es	pcfg	20150108	AnCora 3.0.1	model	86.27	91.32	5.05

Figure 1: Comparison of applying models with broken encoding 1) as-is to a corpus (column *broken*) vs. 2) transforming the corpus tokens to the same broken representation used in the model before applying the model (column *fixed*).

5 Conclusion

In this paper, we have analyzed publicly distributed pre-trained models for NLP tools for issues related to *encoding*, *tokenization*, *normalization*, and *change*. We found several serious flaws which have been communicated to the respective model creators. To support model creators to perform automatic sanity checks on their models and to allow model consumers to get a better understanding of the models they use, we introduce a new tool called *Model Investigator*.

As future work, we plan to extend *Model Investigator* so it can be applied directly to training corpora before creating models. In our opinion, certain normalization steps (e.g. removing SHY or NBSP characters) should rather be fixed in the underlying corpora than during training or processing. Due to the frequency cutoff often used when training models, systematic issues on low-frequency tokens may go unnoticed and analyzing the corpora directly may, thus, reveal additional issues. Finally, more checks should be implemented to investigate deeper into potential source of problems raised by the increasing use of Unicode. For example, it should be investigated whether homoglyphs in Unicode (e.g. different dashes) are problematic.

Our techniques can also be embedded e.g. into UIMA or GATE tool wrappers to dynamically configure normalization steps or make up for bad encoding. This is another area we plan to investigate further in future work.

Acknowledgments

This work has received funding from the European Union's Horizon 2020 research and innovation programme (H2020-EINFRA-2014-2) under grant agreement No. 654021. It reflects only the author's views and the EU is not liable for any use that may be made of the information contained therein. It was further supported by the German Federal Ministry of Education and Research (BMBF) under the promotional reference 01UG1416B (CEDIFOR).

---

[8]The AnCora corpus is missing POS tags in several cases. To train the Spanish CoreNLP models, a heuristic was applied to fill in missing POS tags. It is implemented in the CoreNLP class *SpanishXMLTreeReader*. We used the same heuristic to fill in missing POS tags during evaluation.

References

Sabine Brants, Stefanie Dipper, Silvia Hansen, Wolfgang Lezius, and George Smith. 2002. The TIGER treebank. In *Proceedings of the Workshop on Treebanks and Linguistic Theories (TLT02)*, pages 24–41, Sozopol, Bulgaria, September.

Hamish Cunningham, Diana Maynard, Kalina Bontcheva, Valentin Tablan, Niraj Aswani, Ian Roberts, Genevieve Gorrell, Adam Funk, Angus Roberts, Danica Damljanovic, Thomas Heitz, Mark A. Greenwood, Horacio Saggion, Johann Petrak, Yaoyong Li, and Wim Peters. 2011. *Text Processing with GATE (Version 6)*.

Rebecca Dridan and Stephan Oepen. 2012. Tokenization: Returning to a long solved problem – a survey, contrastive experiment, recommendations, and toolkit. In *Proceedings of ACL-2012*, pages 378–382, Jeju Island, Korea, July. ACL.

Richard Eckart de Castilho and Iryna Gurevych. 2014. A broad-coverage collection of portable nlp components for building shareable analysis pipelines. In *Proceedings of OIAF4HLT*, pages 1–11, Dublin, Ireland, August. ACL and Dublin City University.

David Ferrucci and Adam Lally. 2004. UIMA: An Architectural Approach to Unstructured Information Processing in the Corporate Research Environment. *Natural Language Engineering*, 10(3-4):327–348, September.

Marie Hinrichs, Thomas Zastrow, and Erhard Hinrichs. 2010. WebLicht: Web-based LRT Services in a Distributed eScience Infrastructure. In Nicoletta Calzolari, Khalid Choukri, Bente Maegaard, Joseph Mariani, Jan Odijk, Stelios Piperidis, Mike Rosner, and Daniel Tapias, editors, *Proceedings of LREC-2010*, pages 489–493, Valletta, Malta, May. ELRA.

Nancy Ide, James Pustejovsky, Christopher Cieri, Eric Nyberg, Di Wang, Keith Suderman, Marc Verhagen, and Jonathan Wright. 2014. The Language Application Grid. In Nicoletta Calzolari, Khalid Choukri, Thierry Declerck, Hrafn Loftsson, Bente Maegaard, Joseph Mariani, Asuncion Moreno, Jan Odijk, and Stelios Piperidis, editors, *Proceedings of LREC-2014*, Reykjavik, Iceland, May. ELRA.

Emanuele Lapponi, Erik Velldal, Nikolay A. Vazov, and Stephan Oepen. 2013. Towards large-scale language analysis in the cloud. In *Proceedings of the workshop on Nordic language research infrastructure at NODAL-IDA 2013; NEALT Proceedings Series 20*, number 89, pages 1–10, Oslo, Norway, July. Linköping University Electronic Press.

Christopher Manning, Mihai Surdeanu, John Bauer, Jenny Finkel, Steven Bethard, and David McClosky. 2014. The Stanford CoreNLP Natural Language Processing Toolkit. In *Proceedings of ACL-2014*, pages 55–60, Baltimore, Maryland, USA, June. Association for Computational Linguistics.

Mitchell P. Marcus, Mary Ann Marcinkiewicz, and Beatrice Santorini. 1993. Building a large annotated corpus of English: the Penn Treebank. *Comput. Linguist.*, 19(2):313–330, June.

Helmut Schmid. 1994. Probabilistic part-of-speech tagging using decision trees. In *Proceedings of International Conference on New Methods in Language Processing*, pages 44–49, Manchester, UK.

Mariona Taulé, M. Antònia Martí, and Marta Recasens. 2008. AnCora: Multilevel annotated corpora for Catalan and Spanish. In Nicoletta Calzolari, Khalid Choukri, Bente Maegaard, Joseph Mariani, Jan Odijk, Stelios Piperidis, and Daniel Tapias, editors, *Proceedings of LREC-2008*, Marrakech, Morocco, May. ELRA. http://www.lrec-conf.org/proceedings/lrec2008/.

Heike Telljohann, Erhard Hinrichs, and Sandra Kübler. 2004. The TüBa-D/Z treebank: Annotating German with a context-free backbone. In *Proceedings of LREC-2004*, pages 2229–2235, Lisbon, Portugal.

Combining Human Inputters and Language Services to provide Multi-language support system for International Symposiums

Takao Nakaguchi
Graduate School of Informatics
Kyoto University
nakaguchi@i.kyoto-u.ac.jp

Masayuki Otani
Graduate School of Informatics
Kyoto University
m-otani@i.kyoto-u.ac.jp

Toshiyuki Takasaki
NPO Pangaea,
Graduate School of Informatics
Kyoto University
toshi@pangaean.org

Toru Ishida
Graduate School of Informatics
Kyoto University
ishida@i.kyoto-u.ac.jp

Abstract

In this research, we introduce and implement a method that combines human inputters and machine translators. When the languages of the participants vary widely, the cost of simultaneous translation becomes very high. However, the results of simply applying machine translation to speech text do not have the quality that is needed for real use. Thus, we propose a method that people who understand the language of the speaker cooperate with a machine translation service in support of multilingualization by the co-creation of value. We implement a system with this method and apply it to actual presentations. While the quality of direct machine translations is 1.84 (fluency) and 2.89 (adequacy), the system has corresponding values of 3.76 and 3.85.

1   Introduction

Multi-language support is used to reduce the language barriers in international symposia whose participants come from various countries and who speak different languages. The de facto multi-language support tool is simultaneous translation by human translators. Simultaneous translation is a very demanding task, especially between languages with different structures like Japanese and English, and costs are high because it takes long time to train the translators. In simultaneous translation, translators listen to the speech, translate the text, and then speak the translation result while closely following the speaker. Several studies have attempted to replace human translators with relatively low cost systems. Automatic speech recognition (ASR) performs the listening task, machine translation the translation task, and speech synthesis performs the speaking task; speech translation technologies like VoiceTra can perform all tasks. Because machine translation receives text as its input, several captioning schemes, which are normally to allow the deaf and hard of hearing to join in the dialogue, can be candidates for performing the listening task. Figure 1 shows the relationships among these technologies.

Translators convert the speech of the speaker directly into a language some of the audience can understand. Trying to provide complete translation coverage for all speaker/audience combinations is impractically expensive and it may impossible to find translators for some minor languages. One solution is using machines to replace or partly replace the translators. The first challenge is the creating inputs that suit the machine translation (MT) service. MT is widely available at reasonable cost and MT results can be given to the audience as text (text to speech (TTS) systems are also possible). Unfortunately, translation quality is very sensitive to the input material. Given that speeches at public meetings tend to be rather extemporaneous and not so fluent, we need to pre-edit the source text to suit the capabilities of the machine translation service if we are to get good quality. Thus, we propose the method that could combines the listening task with MT. We implement the method in a system that is put into practice in two real fields: presentations at an international convention and presentations at a laboratory. This paper introduces related works, describes our method and our implementation of a multi-language support system, explains how it was put into practice, evaluates and discusses the results.

Proceedings of WLSI/OIAF4HLT,
pages 28–35, Osaka, Japan, December 12 2016.

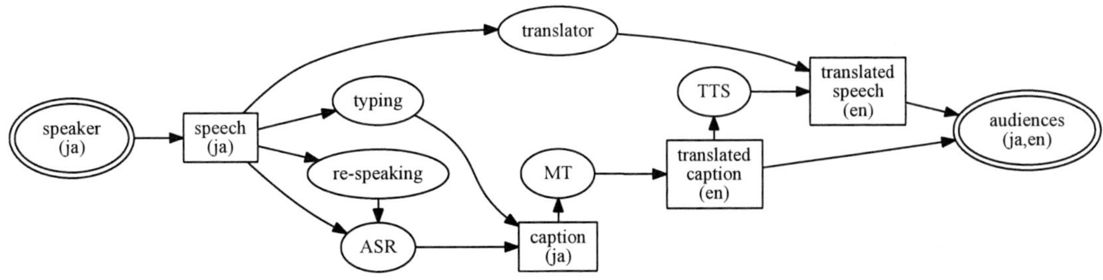

Figure 1: Methods to realize multi-lingualization of speech.

2 Related works

Several research projects have tackled speech captioning in real time. ASR is a technology with a long history, but because ASR accuracy is low, we need to train a recognition model, set-up a low-noise environment or use another person to re-speak the text (Miyoshi et al., 2008) to achieve adequate ASR accuracy.

Captioning is a manual way of creating text from speech. The captionist hears the speech and types it into a computer. To achieve adequate speed, the captionist must be well-trained and use a special keyboard, like a steganography keyboard, so costs get high. To reduce this, *SCRIBE* (Lasecki et al., 2012) proposed to use crowd sourcing for captioning. They divide the speech voice data into small parts, send them to many captionists and merge their outputs. This eases the speed requirements. *IPTalk* (Kurita et al., 2013) proposed another method in which several captionist cooperate to input a speech. All captionists hear the same voice data and decide who inputs which part of speech by monitoring what the others are typing by using a type monitor module on the input screen. *SCRIBE* captionists need not be aware of whole speech but can concentrate on that the part of the speech they must input, while each *IPTalk* captionist is aware of the whole speech but input boundaries are decided by predicting the inputs of others.

The goal of this work is to provide near real-time speech translations with high quality and wide coverage at relatively low-cost. To achieve this, we focus on overcoming the problems raised by the target application, MT of symposium speeches. To achieve adequate translation quality, the input text must be recast (pre-edited) to suit the MT service used and then transcribed to allow MT processing. To achieve acceptable quality and speed we modify the cooperative captioning approach.

3 Problems of multi-lingual support for international symposium

A key problem is that the sentences uttered in symposia tend to be longer and more ambiguous than those in printed texts. The value of pre-editing as a preliminary step to MT has been confirmed for many languages including English(Jachmann, Grabowski and Kudo., 2014), French(Bouillon et al., 2014) and Japanese(Miyata et al., 2015). However, the studies published to date apply pre-editing to written texts, not to spoken text. Accordingly, we evaluated the quality of translation with or without pre-editing of speech material to confirm the effectiveness of pre-editing. Table 1 shows the results. We used *IPTalk*, a cooperative input method, to do caption the speech and *JServer* in the Language Grid(Ishida, 2011) (Murakami et al., 2012) to translate Japanese into English and Chinese. We evaluated fluency and adequacy based on the method written in the evaluation guideline(Linguistic Data Consortium, 2002).

As the translation inputs, we created sentences by concatenating *IPTalk* outputs and creating sentences by setting periods. As evaluation metrics we used fluency, adequacy and concept preservation ratio; maximum score (best) is 5 and minimum (worse) is 1. We also calculated word accuracy (WA) and concept preservation rate to determine how well the surface meaning and intent of the speech text were

Table 1: Translation quality from Japanese speech dictation by cooperative input with or without preedit.

sentence creation method	number of sentence	WA	concept saving rate	target language	average fluency	average adequacy
cooperated captioning	22	79.98	4.8	Chinese	1.77	2.68
				English	1.91	3.09
pre-editing afterward	40	42.63	4	Chinese	3.13	3.70
				English	3.18	3.25

retained. We did morphological analysis by applying *Mecab* to the *IPTalk* outputs (real-time input was given) and the resulting transcript. WA was calculated by the following formula.

$$WA = 1 - \frac{S + D + I}{N}$$

N denotes the number of words in final transcript, S denotes the number of replaced words, D denotes the number of deleted words and I denotes the number of inserted words relative to real-time input. In captioning, the inputters basically enter the words exactly as spoken, but may delete redundant words, shorten sentences or insert words to allow easier comprehension when read. In terms of modifications there were 56 replacements, 126 deletions, and 9 insertions. Concept preservation rate indicates how well the original concepts were expressed by the final transcript (evaluated by Japanese native speakers). The results in Table 1 show that simply applying MT to *IPTalk* output does not yield good translation quality and we can improve the quality by pre-editing the MT inputs.

4 Online Multi-lingual Discussion Tool (OMDT)

Though existing studies considered only static text and not real-time speech texts, the simple modification of simply shortening the text is known to be effective for improving translation quality. From this viewpoint, we design a system that helps inputters to transcribe and pre-edit speech texts for creating MT inputs.

The key components of our system are *Input Screen, Collaboration Server,* and *Display Screen. Input Screen* is one screen of *OMDT* and inputters use this screen to input speech text. This screen runs on a web browser and we can open this screen as necessary to support inputters and languages. The screen also has the ASR Client function to recognize speech by using ASR services on the Cloud. *OMDT* currently supports IBM, Google and Julius ASR engines. The result of ASR and typed entries are shared between *Input Screen*s and *Display Screen*s via the *Collaboration Server*. The *Collaboration Server* is responsible for message transfer among screens and invocation of the composite translation service. When the server receives typed text from the *Input Screen*, the server invokes DictTrans service to translate it. Though our system can access any translation service on *Language Grid*, we usually use DictTrans as it offers a bilingual dictionary. DictTrans combines translation service, bilingual dictionary service and morphological analysis service and can replace/modify special words in the dictionary to enhance translation quality. The server sends the translation result to the user screens. *Display Screen* shows the typed text and the translation result. That screen can show the results of several languages together and also we can open several screens to show many languages. In addition, *Collaboration Server* supports *IPTalk* as the input interface, so inputters can use it instead of the *Input Screen*.

Figure 2 shows one instantiation of our system. This construction is for translating Japanese speech to English at a symposium that has Japanese speakers with Japanese and English audiences. The ASR result is sent to the *Input Screen*s for input processing as shown in Figure 3. *Input Screen* has several display components: Log area, Back translation, Type monitor and Input area in addition to ASR results. Log area shows the input history for the speech, Back translation shows the result of back translation of the text of Input area, Type monitor shows the typing state of other inputters and Input area shows the text currently being pre-edited.

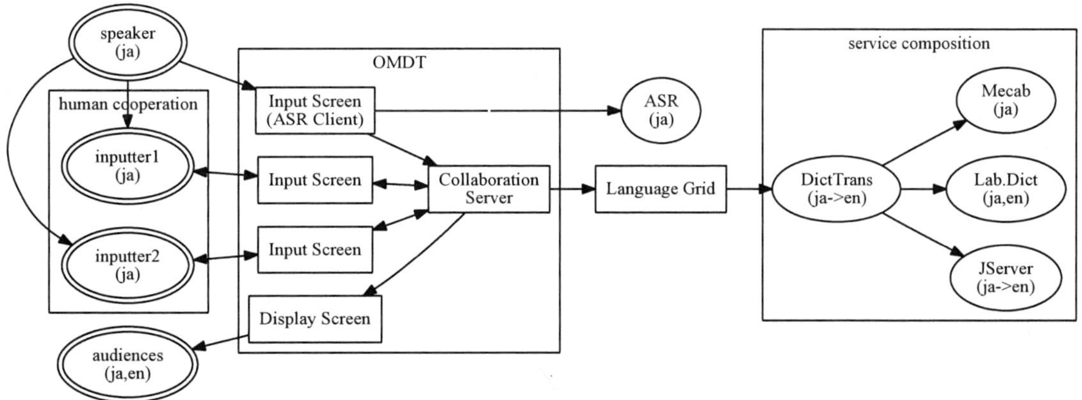

Figure 2: Example construction of whole system

Translated text is finally shown to the audience on the *Display Screen* as shown in Figure 4. We can increase the number of *Input Screens* and *Display Screens* to cover more languages. We can also increase the number of translation pairs the system can translate by adding translation settings (how to combine language services for specific translation pairs) by using *Language Grid*.

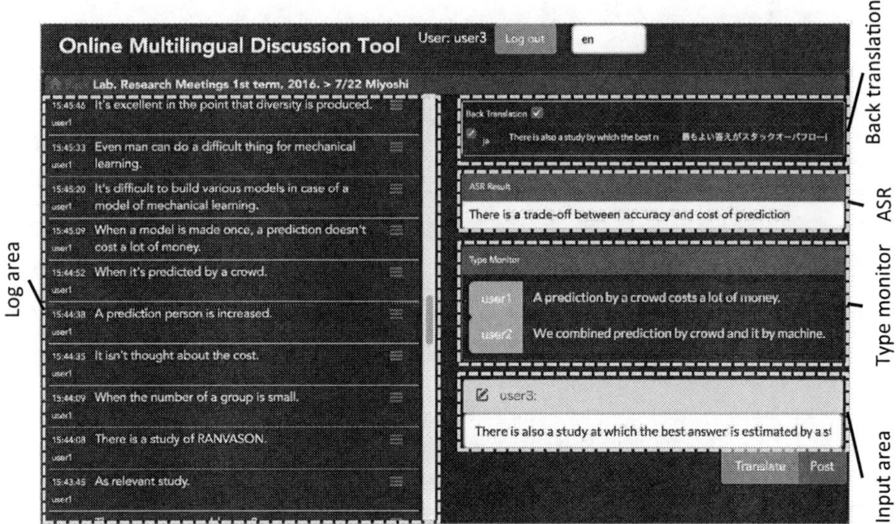

Figure 3: Input screen

5   Take the system into real use

5.1   Practice 1: International Symposium

We applied our system in an international symposium. Two inputters were used (Inputter A and B) and their mother language was Japanese. To achieve adequate input speed, both were experienced in data input work and to maximize translation quality, we trained them in pre-editing and the use of *IPTalk* beforehand. For training, we had them perform, independently, three trial in 90 minutes. In each trial they listened to and pre-edited speech (in Japanese) and then checked the translation result. Next, the inputters

Lab. Research Meetings 1st term, 2016.

日本語	English
自然言語処理の応用では何がなされているか *(original)*	What is formed out of the applicability of the natural-language processing? *(translated)*
やってみないとわからないので、はっきりと言えない *(original)*	I don't find out that it won't be tried, so you can't say clearly. *(translated)*
ディープラーニングは人間のわからない特徴量には効果的だと思うが，今回のケースでも効果がある *(original)*	I think Deep learning is effective in the feature quantity man doesn't know, but is this case *(translated)*

Figure 4: Display screen

Figure 5: The look of conference hall

worked together in performing five trials in five hours. In the training sessions, inputter A entered 495 sentences while B entered 481. We provided multi-language support for Y's Men International 26th Asia Area Convention. This symposium drew 962 participants and was held over three days in Kyoto, Japan. Figure 5 shows a picture of the conference hall. We used our system to provide real-time multi-language translation for an 80 minute Japanese speech. The hall has three screens. The center screen shows the live video or slides as determined by the presenter, left screen displayed Japanese text and English translation and right screen displayed Japanese text and Chinese translation. 738 sentences were input, translated and displayed during the speech.

The system consisted of one server machine (MacBook), two machines to display the translations (Windows) and two machines to run *IPTalk* (used in the training sessions); all machines were notebook PCs.

5.2 Practice2: Presentation at laboratory

We also applied our system to a 30 minute presentation in our laboratory. The audience consisted of 20 people. There were two inputters and the two speakers used English. The system translated the speech into Vietnamese, Chinese, Dutch, Japanese and Korean. Two screens were used; the left one displayed the first three languages and the right one for the last two languages.

The system for this support consisted of one server (MacBook), two machines for inputters (MacBook) and two machines for displaying translation (Windows). We used one web screen of our system as the em Input Screen. Both inputters had no experience in captioning but we trained them for two hours (input

Table 2: Status of input of multilingual support

Inputter / Question	Exp.1(ja)		Exp.2(en)	
	A	B	C	D
Number of input sentences	290	448	94	76
Ave. number of characters	12.8	10.8		
Ave. numbers of words			6.68	7.7
Miss-inputs(%)	4(1.38)	1(0.22)	4(4.26)	2(2.63)
Redundant inputs(%)	7(2.41)	11(2.46)	0(0)	1(1.32)
Succession inputs(%)	32(11.03)	191(42.63)	36(38.3)	19(25)

Table 3: The questionnaire of inputter(1:worst-5:best)

Inputter / Question	Exp.1(ja)		Exp.2(en)	
	A	B	C	D
Was the input screen easy to look at?			4	4
Was the Back translation useful?			4	4
Was the Type monitor useful?			5	5
Was the whole input function easy to use?			4	3
Was the IPTalk easy to use?	4	4		
Could you cooperate other inputter well?	5	4	4	5
Could you input whole speech?	4	4	3	3

separately for 30 minutes and input cooperatively for one and half hours) beforehand. 170 sentences were inputted, translated and displayed during the presentation.

6 Results and discussions

6.1 Questionnaire

Table 2 shows the details of inputs in the two experiments. Inputters input in Japanese in Experiment 1 and English in Experiment 2. Average number of characters is the average number of characters per Japanese sentence and average number of words is the average number of words per English sentence. Miss-inputs indicates the number of sentences that have obvious input faults such as "shrae"(should be "share"). Redundant inputs is the number of sentences which are similar to previous input (i.e. one inputter input "from Germany," and the other inputter input "From Germany and Denmark." in succession). Successive inputs is the number of sentences consecutively entered by the same inputter.

We conducted questionnaires after the experiments. Table 3 shows the results of inputters in Exp.1 and Exp.2. The questions examined the functionality or usability of input functions, the cooperation with other inputter, and subjective evaluation of inputters about cover rate; a five-point scale was used. For input functions, we used *IPTalk* in Exp.1 and the *Input Screen* of our system in Exp.2, so questions for Exp.2 include each part of the *Input Screen*. Table 4 shows the impressions of the audience. We asked five questions (five-point response) and totaled the number of people who choose the same point. From Exp. 2, 16 of 20 people in the audience responded. Table 5 shows the translation quality of 50 sentences extracted randomly from Exp.1.

6.2 Input method

We assume inputters of our system would enter sentences by turns by cooperating with each other while the translation service would accept the pre-edited speech to keep translation quality as high as possible. Thus we attempted to train the inputters well beforehand. As Table 2 shows, however, sequential input was common. We considered that turn taking would be naturally selected but in practice the inputters

Table 4: The questionnaire of audience(Exp.2)(1:worst-5:best)

Question	Number of people of each score				
	1	2	3	4	5
Was the translation screen easy to look at?	1	3	2	7	3
Was the translation displayed in a timely manner?	0	6	7	3	0
Was the content of the translation easy to understand?	1	9	5	1	0
Was the content of the translation helpful to understand the presentation?	0	5	5	5	1
Will you want to use this system in the future?	0	2	6	5	3

Table 5: The quality of translation of Exp.1

sentence creation method	number of sentence	target language	average fluency	average adequacy
cooperated pre-editing input	50	Chinese	3.58	3.82
		English	3.94	3.88

sometimes input sentences sequentially.

The inputters' response showed that the systems were viewed very positively by all four inputters (inputter D experienced some difficulty because f his customized keyboard). So we conclude that the input function posed no obvious difficulties to the inputters.

6.3 Translation quality

The shorter training time is preferred because we assume that some of audience become inputter and cooperate each other and translation service, and realize multi-language support. But we need certain length of training because inputters of cooperated pre-editing input must get accustomed to pre-editing and predicting which inputter inputs which part of speech. For Exp.1 we train them six and half hours, and for Exp.2 three hours. Table 5 shows the certain translation quality enhancement, that average fluency improved from 1.84 to 3.76 and average adequacy from 2.89 to 3.76, but the evaluation by audience of Exp.2 was low. Though we could not simply compare the results of each experiments because the language of input and output is different and the speech is also different, at least we can see the result that by training inputters six hours we could get certain translation quality and we could assume that we don't need training and trained skills as simultaneous translators have. But we still need to improve input functions or way to training to reduce training time and advance input efficiency.

7 Conclusion

In this paper, we tried to solve the following problems to realize low cost and high quality multi-language support.

- Translation quality improvement by the cooperation of human inputters and language services.

- Realizing a multi-language support system whose user interface supports inputter cooperation and language services.

The proposed method was shown to improve translation quality by keeping the original intent of the speech; this is done by combining real-time cooperative captioning and pre-editing for input to an MT service. We implemented the multi-language support system and put it into practice in actual international symposium and achieved fluency and adequacy scores of 3.58 and 3.82 for Japanese-Chinese translation, and 3.94 and 3.88 for Japanese-English translation. While the content of speech itself is different between Table 1 and Table 5, the speaker was same. It shows some positive effect of our method.

At the implementation of the system, we developed *Input Screen* that has log area, type monitor and back translation, and *Translation Screen*. By translating speech from Japanese to English and Chinese at Exp.1 and English to five other languages at Exp.2, we show our user interface has some usability by evaluation by users.

Acknowledgements

This work was supported by Grant-in-Aid for Scientific Research (S) (24220002) of Japan Society for the Promotion of Science (JSPS). The authors wish to thank members of Y's men international Asia Area and president Okano for supporting this research.

References

Pierrette Bouillon, Liliana Gaspar, Johanna Gerlach, Victoria Porro, Johann Roturier. 2014. *Pre-editing by Forum Users: a Case Study.* 3-10. Controlled Natural Language Simplifying Language Use.

Torsten Jachmann, Robert Grabowski, and Mayo Kudo. 2014. *Machine-Translating English Forum Posts to Japanese: On Pre-editing Rules as Part of Domain Adaptation.* 20th Annual Meeting. 808-811. Natural Language Processing.

Toru Ishida (Ed.). 2011. *The Language Grid: Service-Oriented Collective Intelligence for Language Resource Interoperability.*, ISBN 978-3-642-21177-5. Springer.

Shigeaki Kurita, Sumihiro Kawano and Keiko Kondou. 2013. *The remote computer assisted speech-to-text interpreter system for reducing operational costs*, vol. 15, no. 8, SIG-ACI-10, 13-20. Human Interface Society.

Walter S. Lasecki, Christopher D. Miller, Adam Sadilek, Andrew Abumoussa, Donato Borrello, Raja Kushalnagar, and Jeffrey P. Bigham. 2012. *Real-Time Captioning by Groups of Non-Experts* Proceedings of the 25th annual ACM symposium on User interface software and technology.

Linguistic Data Consortium. 2002. *Linguistic Data Annotation Specification: Assessment of Fluency and Adequacy in Arabic-English and Chinese-English Translations.*

Robert F. Lusch and Stephen L. Vargo. 2006. *The service dominant logic of marketing: Dialog, debate and directions.* Armonk, NY. M.E. Sharpe.

Shodai Matsuda, Xinhui Hu, and Yoshinori Shiga. 2013. *Multilingual speech-to-speech translation system: Voice-Tra.*, Vol. 2. 14th International Conference on Mobile Data Management (MDM).

Rei Miyata, Anthony Hartley, Cécile Paris, Midori Tatsumi, and Kyo Kageura 2015. *Japanese Controlled Language Rules to Improve Machine Translatability of Municipal Documents.* 90-103. MT Summit XV.

Shigeki Miyoshi, Hayato Kuroki, Sumihiro Kawano, Mayumi Shirasawa, Yasushi Ishihara, Masayuki Kobayashi. 2008. *Support Technique for Real-Time Captionist to Use Speech Recognition Software*, International Conference on Computers for Handicapped Persons. Springer Berlin Heidelberg.

Y. Murakami, M. Tanaka, D. Lin and T. Ishida. 2012. *Service grid federation architecture for heterogeneous domains.* 539-546. IEEE International Conference on Services Computing,

Masahiro Tanaka, Yohei Murakami, Donghui Lin, and Toru Ishida. 2010. *Language Grid Toolbox: Open source multi-language community site.* 4th International Conference on Universal Communication Symposium (IUCS), IEEE.

Recurrent Neural Network with Word Embedding for Complaint Classification

Panuwat Assawinjaipetch, Virach Sornlertlamvanich
School of Information, Computer, and Communication Technology (ICT),
Sirindhorn International Institute of Technology,
Khlong Nung, Khlong Luang District, Pathum Thani, Thailand
panuwat.a@studentmail.siit.tu.ac.th, virach@siit.tu.ac.th

Kiyoaki Shirai	**Sanparith Marukata**
School of Information Science,	National Electronics and Computer Technology Center (NECTEC)
Japan Advanced Institute of Science and Technology (JAIST),	112 Phahonyothin Road, Klong Neung,
1-1 Asahidai, Nomi,	Klong Luang District,
1-2 Ishikawa 923-1292, Japan	Pathumthani, Thailand
kshirai@jaist.ac.jp	**sanparith.marukatat@nectec.or.th**

Abstract

Complaint classification aims at using information to deliver greater insights to enhance user experience after purchasing the products or services. Categorized information can help us quickly collect emerging problems in order to provide a support needed. Indeed, the response to the complaint without the delay will grant users highest satisfaction. In this paper, we aim to deliver a novel approach which can clarify the complaints precisely with the aim to classify each complaint into nine predefined classes i.e. accessibility, company brand, competitors, facilities, process, product feature, staff quality, timing respectively and others. Given the idea that one word usually conveys ambiguity and it has to be interpreted by its context, the word embedding technique is used to provide word features while applying deep learning techniques for classifying a type of complaints. The dataset we use contains 8,439 complaints of one company.

1 Introduction

While Space Vector Model (SVM) with TF-IDF is widely used as a traditional method for text classification, we cannot neglect that the deep learning with word embedding technique outperforms traditional method so far until now in many comparison reports such as sentiment analysis, named entity recognition, semantic relation extraction and so on. It is undeniable truth that word embedding with neural network can be effectively applied to the natural language processing task nowadays with highly accurate results. This is the especially for the Recurrent Neural Network (RNN) which is able to detect the hidden relationship between inputs as well as to provide a precise sequence prediction with the state-of-the-art result in various machine learning domains such as computer vision (L. Yao, 2015) and language modeling (Y. Kim, 2015). Because of the long term dependency detection capability, pattern recognition tasks such as speech recognition (Y. Miao, 2015) and handwriting recognition (A. Graves, 2009) also shown great results when applied with RNN. This paper presents a classification recurrent neural network model that deals with the complaint classification task. The model is compared with TF-IDF, SVM and CBOW methods which are widely used for the text classification. The experiment shows that the model can outperform other methods for the complaint classification significantly.

Proceedings of WLSI/OIAF4HLT,
pages 36–43, Osaka, Japan, December 12 2016.

2   Related works

2.1   Text classification

The collection of complaints is clearly described in negative sense. Hence, sentiment analysis approaches will not work efficiently for this task, especially for the methods which rely on the counts of positive and negative words. The similar work to us is a claim classification introduced by J. Park (2014). The high accuracy model that can distinguish; verifiable with evidence, verifiable without evidence and unverifiable claims, is achieved by using n-gram, handcrafted features and SVM. However, the feature preparing task required prior knowledge of the language. Moreover, the handcrafted features extraction is a very time consuming task and cannot be applied to every language because of the difference between grammars.

2.2   Word2Vec

The word embedding technique recently becomes the most dominant in terms of the power in expanding the meaning of each word by using its co-occurrence statistics of each word. In the previous half decade of the research since R. Collobert (2011), the results show that the word and phrase embeddings significantly boost the performance in many of NLP tasks such as syntactic parsing (D. Zeng, 2014) and sentiment analysis (R. Socher, 2013). Introduced by T. Mikolov (2013), Word2Vec has gained a lot of traction as it takes a very short time for training while providing a high quality of word embeddings information. The tool can be derived into two types that are skip-gram model or continuous bag-of-words model, with an optimization method such as negative sampling or hierarchical softmax. As in the recent research on Word2Vec, we found that skip-gram with negative sampling is the best match to our data as the number of complaints is limited. This model shows a better performance compared to bag-of-words while negative sampling is a most efficient method to derive the word embedding. The objective function (Y. Goldberg, 2014) used to generate the word embedding is described in Equation (1) where w is the words, c is the set of contexts of word w. D is the set of all word and context pairs and D' is a set of randomly negative samples.

$$\arg\max_{\theta} \sum_{(w,c)\in D} \log \sigma(v_c \cdot v_w) + \sum_{(w,c)\in D'} \log \sigma(-v_c \cdot v_w) \tag{1}$$

2.3   Long Short-Term Memory

Considering complaint classification is a sequence prediction, RNN become much useful in terms of discovering the long-term dependencies. However, the learning of long-term dependencies with gradient descent is very difficult as stated by Y. Bengio et al. (1994). The reason occurs from the vanishing gradient problem which causes the backpropagation through time to repeatedly multiply the gradient value. If the amplitude of the gradient is lower than *one* then the repetition of multiplying it will push this value towards *zero*. Therefore, the model cannot learn long-term dependency when we adjust a new value using gradient descent method. LSTM is kind of RNN which has been introduced since 1997 by S. Hochreiter et al. (1997) that prevents vanishing gradient from occurring. For LSTM, Cell state (C_t) are connected to three gates which are forget gate (f_t), input gate (i_t) and output gate (o_t) respectively. Equation used to calculate these gates are shown in Equation (2), (3) and (4) respectively.

$$f_t = \mathrm{sigmoid}(W_f \bullet [h_{t-1}, x_t] + b_f) \tag{2}$$
$$i_t = \mathrm{sigmoid}(W_i \bullet [h_{t-1}, x_t] + b_i) \tag{3}$$
$$\bar{C_t} = \tanh(W_C \bullet [h_{t-1}, x_t] + b_C)$$
$$C_t = f_t * C_{t-1} + i_t * \bar{C_t}$$
$$o_t = \mathrm{sigmoid}(W_o \bullet [h_{t-1}, x_t] + b_o)$$
$$h_t = o_t * \tanh(C_t) \tag{4}$$

2.4   Gated Recurrent Unit

Gate Recurrent Unit is a method proposed recently by K. Cho et al. (2014), with the ability to capture the long-term dependencies as LSTM. Figure 1 shows the difference between GRU and LSTM that GRU uses one less gate than LSTM. LSTM has i, f and o as input, forget and output gates respectively. C and $\bar{C}$ denote the current/new memory cell content. On the other hand, GRU only has r and z as reset and update gates. The h and $\bar{h}$ are the current and candidate activation gates respectively.

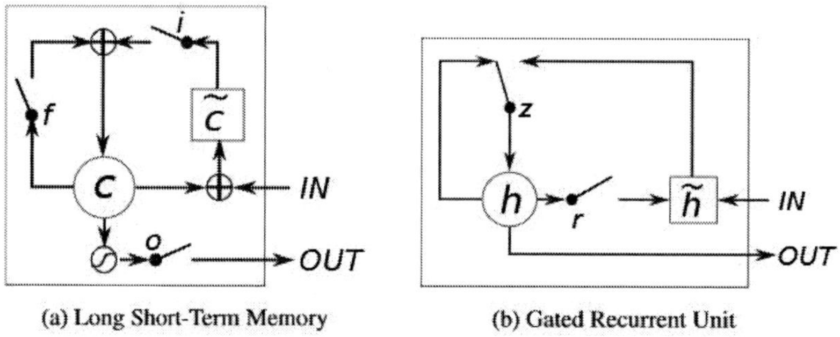

(a) Long Short-Term Memory   (b) Gated Recurrent Unit

Figure 1: Illustration of LSTM and GRU

The model is designed to make each recurrent unit to be able to adaptively capture dependencies in a different time scale. It is similar to LSTM unit by having gating units that calibrate the information flow at the inside unit without creating new memory cells. We can compute updated gate (z), reset gate (r), hidden state (h) and current state (s_t) of the GRU at time t using Equation (5), (6), (7) and (8). For the pros and cons other than GRU has one less gate than LSTM which results that GRU consume less memory, there is no concrete proof shows superiority of one to another.

$$z = \mathrm{sigmoid}(x_t U^z + s_{t-1} W^z) \tag{5}$$

$$r = \mathrm{sigmoid}(x_t U^r + s_{t-1} W^r) \tag{6}$$

$$h = \tanh(x_t U^h + (s_{t-1} \bullet r) W^h) \tag{7}$$

$$s_t = ((1 - z) \bullet h) + (z \bullet s_{t-1}) \tag{8}$$

2.5   Our work

As discussed above, there are several attempts in using the neural network model with word embedding technique for basic task in NLP such as sentiment analysis and syntactic parsing i.e. A. Severyn (2015), C.N. dos Santos (2014) and M. Ghiassi (2013). However, there has a few research works using RNNs (S. Lai, 2015) and Bidirectional RNNs (O. Irsoy, 2014) with word embedding for text classification rather than sentiment analysis. The current research of document classification still mostly uses the so-called TF-IDF as it is a straightforward approach, for example, the word such as *stock* tends to appear more in economic documents than politic documents. Also it can be efficiently implemented and be improved by gathering more data that related to it. However, Word2Vec is believably considered to provide a better word features than TF-IDF.

The sentences are sent as input sequences connected to the embedding layer. Therefore, each word in the sentence is mapped as input sequences for the bidirectional RNN (M. Schuster, 1997). The bidirectional RNN that are our approach consist of *forward-backward GRUs* (gru-gru), *forward-backward LSTM* (lstm-lstm), forward-LSTM backward-GRU (lstm-gru) and forward-GRU and backward-LSTM (gru-lstm). The expectation is that to expose the dependency from both sides, i.e. forward and backward, the bidirectional model can perform better than single direction model. The bidirectional RNN connection shown in Figure 2 is a novel approach based on a combination of an existing model for a new task to overcome the traditional method TF-IDF.

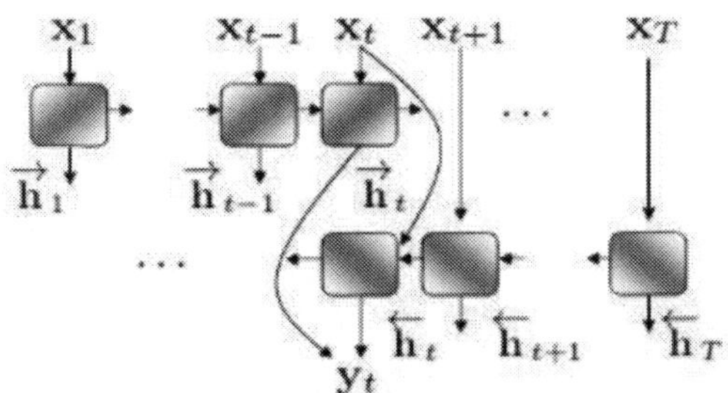

Figure 2: Unfold RNN for bidirectional.

3   Method

In our complaint classification model, the model must be able to distinguish the between nine classes that are *Accessibility*, Company *brand, Competitor, Facility, Process, Product feature, Staff quality, Timing* and *Others*. Each input of the model is a text contains one complaint that is passed through the preprocessing step, embedding step, neural network layer, and max pooling the output to select the category which it belongs to. The complaint classes are defined as following.

    Accessibility is the complaint regarding the rarity to acquire products or services.

    Company brand is the complaint about reliability of the company.

    Competitor is the complaint that mentions about the business competitor in terms of comparison.

    Facility is a complaint related to the difficulty from the uses of products or services.

    Process is a complaint about the complexity of the procedure.

    Product feature is a complaint about promotions or privileges.

    Staff quality is a complaint about human resource in the department.

    Timing is a complaint about the waiting time during using products or receiving services.

    Others are complaints which could not be classified in any group.

    Our proposed method consists of the word segmentation, word representation generating and neural network modules that are sequentially applied.

3.1   Word Segmentation

Thai language has no punctuation marks and no spacing in a sentence. So in the preprocessing step, *word segmentation* is one of the most crucial steps needed in order to be able to generate an input for Word2Vec. The successfully preprocessing result can lead to a high accurate word unit which is used to generate the word representation. On the other hand, the low accurate preprocessing results in a low accurate word representation and deteriorate a prediction model trained in the succeeding steps. Our preprocessing uses the existing dictionary to handle the word segmentation with error handling expression such as typos prevention, unnecessary symbols and whitespaces removing.

3.2   Word Representation Generating

After the *word segmentation,* Word2Vec is applied to obtain word embedding. The setting used here is three negative sampling, 64 hidden units, and the frequency required for a word to be reserved in the dictionary is two. Skip bi-gram method is applied as we have only 8,439 sentences, which are not effective enough for CBOW to generate a highly accurate word representation. In addition, if the accuracy of the word representation is good, the words which have similar meaning and similar usage must have almost the same vector representation, as shown in Table 1 where '*the*' and '*a*' having almost the same vector.

Index	Input	Array [0 ...... n]		
0	the	0.13	0.11	0.13
1	a	0.17	0.12	0.11
2	responsive	0.33	0.25	0.77
3	slow	0.21	0.66	0.99

Table 1: Index mapping to the word and array representing each word.

3.3   Neural Network Layer

RNNs are introduced in our approach, it is important to keep input as a matrix shaped fit for training. The output from Word2Vec looks like a dictionary of each word mapped to a list of array.

The complaint sentences are usually not very long so we can take the longest sentence to determine the maximum number of word in a sentence. The sentences which are shorter than the maximum length must be padded[1] to make it become 30 words sentence. Then we map these words to embedding layer and connect it directly to a hidden layer of 64 units of neural network models i.e. *fnn*, *gru*, *lstm*, *gru-gru*, *lstm-gru*, *gru-lstm* and *lstm-lstm*. Finally, the outputs from our hidden layer are connected to the softmax layer of predefined classes on top, of it as the shown in Figure 3.

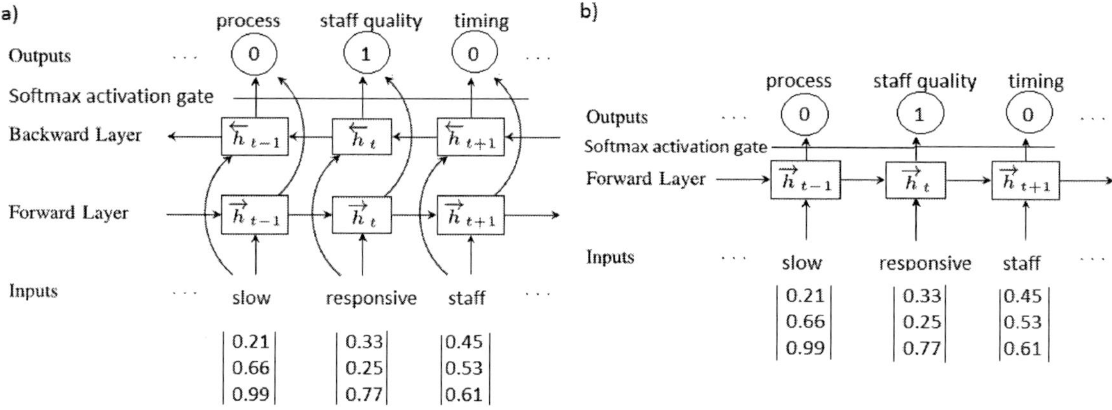

Figure 3: a) Bidirectional LSTM/GRU. b) Single direction LSTM/GRU architectures for 9-classes complaint classification.

4   Experiment

To conduct an empirical evaluation of our proposed method, we compare it with the traditional TF-IDF model and also other popular machine learning model such as Feedforward Neural Network (FNN), LSTM and also try with a different combination of LSTM and GRU with the same training and test set.

F1 score is used to evaluate our result. With our data about 8,439 complaints annotated in nine classes, we separate our data into 80% and 20% for training and testing respectively. Therefore, we have 6,755 and 1,684 sentences for using in training set and test set respectively.

By using Bag-of-Words with TF-IDF, we can get the F1 score for prediction reach only about 75%, which all of Embedding Layer with Neural Network hidden layer can completely surpass this F1 score after a few epochs of training.

For the other models which are based on neural network, we first provide the same initial weight for each word by using Word2Vec for representing each word in our embedding layer. The weight of unknown word is obtained by replacing rare words to unknown word in the corpus before passing those rare words into Word2Vec as we cannot obtain many information from the word that rarely appear in a corpus. As a result, we could obtain a well-balanced weight for unknown word. As the training set is not a very big corpus and the number of vocabularies is not quite high, the more dimensions for word embedding seem to cause the extremely varying vector of similar words. The best word   embed-

[1]Bucketing and Padding idea from: https://www.tensorflow.org/versions/r0.10/tutorials/seq2seq/index.html

ding we can achieve is obtained by using 100 dimensions for word embedding with ADAM (D. Kingma, 2014) optimization.

After running both training and test sets with *fnn* with 64 hidden units, the highest accuracy on training set can almost get a perfect score on training set with a fastest convergence, but, for a test set, it barely passed 80% which given the lowest F1 score among all other neural network models. By increasing the number of hidden units, the gap of F1 score between training set and test set keeps increasing.

LSTM and GRU are experimented with the same number of hidden units. The F1 score of the prediction is clearly better than MLP. There is no doubt that it can find a long term dependency between words. In addition, the model is able to Figure out some combination order of words used to classify an output class. Also, it seems likely that GRU converges a little bit faster than LSTM, while the prediction is almost on par, but much more stable for a long term training as shown in Figure 4a.

model	Best prediction on test set			epoch	Result prediction on test set avg.		
	p	r	f1	no.	p	r	f1
fnn	**0.859**	**0.856**	**0.857**	**9**	0.824	0.828	0.826
gru	0.847	0.845	0.846	50	0.827	0.825	0.826
lstm	0.857	0.855	0.856	17	**0.837**	**0.834**	**0.835**
gru-gru	0.853	0.850	0.851	30	0.833	0.832	0.833
lstm-gru	0.852	0.842	0.847	13	0.820	0.825	0.822
gru-lstm	0.853	0.849	0.851	13	0.819	0.822	0.820
lstm-lstm	0.852	0.848	0.850	41	0.834	0.830	0.832

Table 2: Comparison result of NN model between best and average results.

Furthermore, *the lstm-lstm, gru-gru, lstm-gru* and *gru-lstm* combinations are experimented in bidirectional architectures phase. The bidirectional GRU and LSTM are converged faster and more accurate than the composition between LSTM and GRU. Also, the F1 score is same as a single direction LSTM or GRU. However, the bidirectional models sometime provide better results than the single direction average results and also converge much faster as shown in Figure 4b.

Table 2 shows that all of our approach with Neural Network model has surpassed the baseline set by TF-IDF which is 75% with no difficulty. It is our concrete evidence that the word embedding provides more information for the model to be able to detect dependencies used for classifying the document. Moreover, the FNN can achieve best prediction result after a few epochs of training but self-declining from an overfitting effect is inevitable after continuous training. The GRU recurrent neural network has the most stability in maintaining its states once it converged. Also, it converges much faster than LSTM. However, in a long-term training, the result of LSTM seems to be better. The bidirectional model seems not to be very convinced. But, it is still too soon to conclude that backward dependency detection is unnecessary. In the Figure 4, it can be seen that the model which uses a bidirectional GRU or LSTM can converge much faster than the single direction GRU/LSTM. A comparison of F1 score between *fnn* (red), *lstm* (green) and *gru* (blue) for training set (higher line) and test set (lower line) is shown in Figure 4a. Also, the comparison of F1 score between l*stm-gru* (blue), *lstm-lstm* (green), *gru-lstm* (red) and *gru-gru* (violet) for training set (higher line) and test set (lower line) is shown in Figure 4b.

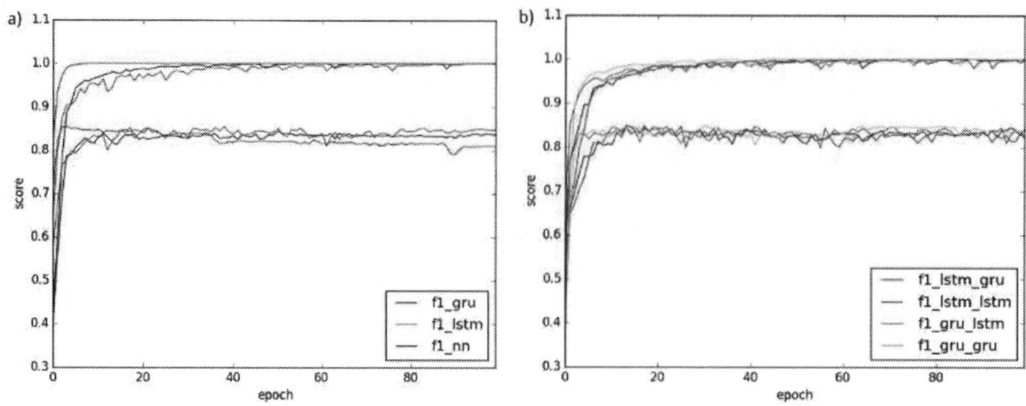

Figure 4: Comparison of F1 score. a) FNN, LSTM and GRU. b) Combination of LSTM-GRU

5   Conclusion

In this paper, we present the word embedding used for complaint classification which combine with recurrent neural network LSTM and GRU with a single direction and also bidirectional. Our evaluation focuses on the comparison of F1 score between various combinations of bidirectional LSTM-GRU. Bidirectional recurrent neural network can surpass the traditional method, TF-IDF (75% F1 score) while using the same amount of training data. The usage time for training is dependent upon the processing unit. It requires about 2-3 hours for the training with a graphic processing unit NVIDIA 660M with 8 GB RAM with 64 word dimensions and 64 hidden units for each architecture. But the execution time requires a few second to predict each sentence.

The bidirectional model tends to work better when it is combined with the same kind of network. We consider this approach as our preliminary step for extending our research further to have better understanding in bidirectional GRU and LSTM characteristic.

Although, bidirectional approach shows no significant result comparing to those single direction GRU and LSTM, but it converges much faster. We also found that the misclassification occurs from the multi-class relevance sentence such as *'The staff has a low responsiveness which results in the process took so long'*. The problem defined here is one of our consideration to replace the last activation layer of the model with *sigmoid* function instead of *softmax* function.

So, it is still too early to decide that the backward dependency is completely not needed. The model improvement could be achieved by an increment of corpus and a better preprocessing step. The recursive neural network is also one of our options, as it shows a very good result in a sentiment analysis task recently.

6   Acknowledgement

This research is financially supported by National Science and Technology Development Agency (NSTDA), National Electronics and Computer Technology Center (NECTEC), Japan Advanced Institute of Technology (JAIST), Sirindhorn International Institute of Technology (SIIT), Thammasat University (TU). Also, special thanks to Feedback180 Co., Ltd. for the corpus and verification of the experiment correctness.

References

L. Yao, A. Torabi, K. Cho, N. Ballas, C. Pal, H. Larochelle, A. Courville. 2015. *Describing videos by exploiting temporal structure*. In Proceedings of the IEEE International Conference on Computer Vision. pages 4507–4515.

Y. Kim, Y. Jernite, D. Sontag, A. M. Rush. 2015. *Character-aware neural language models*. arXiv:1508.06615.

Y. Miao, M. Gowayyed, F. Metze. Eesen. 2015. *End-to-end speech recognition using deep rnn models and wfst-based decoding*. arXiv:1507.08240.

A. Graves, M. Liwicki, S. Fernandez, R. Bertolami, H. Bunke, J. Schmidhuber. 2009. *A Novel Connectionist System for Improved Unconstrained Handwriting Recognition*. IEEE Transactions on Pattern Analysis and Machine Intelligence, vol. 31, no. 5.

T. Mikolov, K. Chen, G. Corrado, and J. Dean. 2013. *Efficient estimation of word representations in vector space*. arXiv:1301.3781.

S. Hochreiter, Y. Bengio, P. Frasconi, J. Schmidhuber. 2001. *Gradient flow in recurrent nets: the difficulty of learning long-term dependencies*. In S. C. Kremer and J. F. Kolen, editors, A Field Guide to Dynamical Recurrent Neural Networks. IEEE.

J. Park, C. Cardie. 2014. *Identifying Appropriate Support for Propositions in Online User Comments*. Proceedings of the First Workshop on Argumentation Mining, pages 29–38, Baltimore, Maryland USA.

R. Socher, J. Bauer, C. D. Manning, A. Y. Ng. 2013. *Parsing with Compositional Vector Grammars*. ACL.

R. Socher, A. Perelygin, J. Y. Wu, J. Chuang, C. D. Manning, A. Y. Ng, C. Potts. 2013. *Recursive Deep Models for Semantic Compositionality Over a Sentiment Treebank*. EMNLP.

D. Zeng, K. Liu, S. Lai, G. Zhou, J. Zhao. 2014. *Relation Classification via Convolutional Deep Neural Network*. In Proceedings of the 25th International Conference on Computational Linguistics (COLING), pages 2335–2344, Dublin, Ireland.

Y. Bengio, P. Simard, and P. Frasconi. 1994. *Learning Long-Term Dependencies with Gradient Descent is Difficult*. IEEE Transaction on Neural Network. Vol. 5, No. 2.

S. Hochreiter, J. Schmidhuber. Long Short-Term Memory. Neural Computation 9 (8): 1735-1780, 1997.

K. Cho, B. van Merrienboer, D. Bahdanau, and Y. Bengio. 2014. *On the properties of neural machine translation: Encoder-decoder approaches*. arXiv:1409.1259.

M. Schuster, K. K. Paliwal. 1997. *Bidirectional Recurrent Neural Networks*. IEEE Transaction on signal processing. vol. 45. No. 11.

D. P. Kingma, J. L. Ba. 2015. *ADAM: A method for stochastic optimization*. ICLR 2015. arXiv:1412.6980.

R. Collobert, J. Weston, L. Bottou, M. Karlen, K. Kavukcuoglu, P. Kuksa. 2011. *Natural Language Processing (Almost) from Scratch*. Journal of Machine Learning Research, 12:2493-2537.

Y. Goldberg and Omer Levy. 2014. *word2vec explained: deriving mikolov et al.'s negative sampling word-embedding method*. arXiv:1402.3722.

S. Lai, L. Xu, K. Liu, J. Zhao. 2015. *Recurrent Convolutional Neural Networks for Text Classification*. In Proc. Conference of the Association for the Advancement of Artificial Intelligence (AAAI).

O. Irsoy, C. Cardie. 2014. *Opinion Mining with Deep Recurrent Neural Networks*. In Proceedings of the 2014 Conference on Empirical Methods in Natural Language Processing (EMNLP), pp. 720–728, Doha, Qatar. Association for Computational Linguistics.

C. N. dos Santos, Cicero, M. Gatti. 2014. *Deep convolutional neural networks for sentiment analysis of short texts*. In Proceedings of COLING 2014, the 25th International Conference on Computational Linguistics: Technical Papers, pp. 69–78.

A. Severyn, A. Moschitti. 2015. *Twitter sentiment analysis with deep convolutional neural networks*. In Proceedings of the 38th International ACM SIGIR Conference on Research and Development in Information Retrieval. pages 959–962.

M. Ghiassi, J. Skinner, D. Zimbra. 2013. *Twitter brand sentiment analysis: A hybrid system using n-gram analysis and dynamic artificial neural network*. Expert Systems with Applications vol. 40, page 6266–6282.

Universal dependencies for Uyghur

Mairehaba Aili
Xinjiang University,China
marhaba@xju.edu.cn

Weinila Mushajiang
Xinjiang University,China
winira@xju.edu.cn

Tuergen Yibulayin
Xinjiang University, China
turgun@xju.edu.cn

Kahaerjiang A.
Xinjiang University
kaharjan@xju.edu.cn

Yan Liu
Xinjiang University
liuyuxiu@xju.edu.cn

Abstract

The Universal Dependencies (UD) Project seeks to build a cross-lingual studies of treebanks, linguistic structures and parsing. Its goal is to create a set of multilingual harmonized treebanks that are designed according to a universal annotation scheme. In this paper, we report on the conversion of the Uyghur dependency treebank to a UD version of the treebank which we term the Uyghur Universal Dependency Treebank (UyDT). We present the mapping of the Uyghur dependency treebank's labelling scheme to the UD scheme, along with a clear description of the structural changes required in this conversion.

1   Introduction

Treebanks can be used for statistical learning as well as evaluation and are available for an increasing number of languages. For instances: Czech (Hajičová, 1998), Danish (Kromann, 2003), Turkish (Oflazer, 2003) Slovene (Džeroski et al., 2006), and Finnish (Haverinen et al., 2010). However, because of having been built with language-related specific schema, it leads to different treebanks with different structure. It seems reasonable, but this has hampered to perform sound comparative evaluations and cross-lingual learning experiments. It is reported that statistical parser output in one language cannot be easily compared or transferred to another when using two training data which labelled with different annotation schemes (McDonald et al, 2011; Søgaard, 2011). Mcdonald et al. (2013) reported improved results on cross-lingual transfer parsing using 10 uniformly annotated treebanks.

The Universal Dependencies (UD) seeks to develop cross-linguistically consistent treebank annotation guidelines and apply them to many languages to create treebank annotations, aiming to capture similarities as well as idiosyncrasies among typologically different languages, and released guideline to assist with the creation of new UD treebanks, or mapping and conversions of existing treebanks to a new universal scheme. The UD scheme is built on the Google Universal part-of-speech (POS) tagset (Petrov et al., 2012), the interset interlingua of morphosyntactic features (Zeman, 2008), and Stanford Dependencies(Tsarfaty, 2013; de Marneffe et al., 2014). In addition to the abstract annotation scheme, UD defines also a treebank storage format, CoNLL-U. The UD scheme accounts for varying linguistic differences across language by providing the option of defining language–specific label sub-types when the prescribed list of labels do not adequately cover all linguistic features of a given language. Nivre (2015) explains the motivation behind the project. Since then, a large number of additional treebanks have been either built or converted from existing treebanks to form new UD treebanks. To date, there are 54 treebanks representing 40 languages listed in the UD project.

We have mapped the Uyghur dependency Treebank (UyDT) (S.Mamitimin et al., 2013; M.Aili et al., 2016) to the UD scheme (Version 1) for purposes of cross-lingual studies and parser improvement. The UyDT is a corpus of Uyghur sentences that have been annotated manually. This paper summarizes the conversion and mapping of the UyDT to Uyghur Universal Dependency Treebank (UyUD), as part of the Universal Dependencies (UD) Project.

Proceedings of WLSI/OIAF4HLT,
pages 44–50, Osaka, Japan, December 12 2016.

2   Brief introduction for UyDT

Uyghur is a Ural-Altaic language, has rich and complex morphological structure. As a typical agglutinative language, Uyghur displays rather different characteristics compared to those more well-studied languages in the parsing literature. On the syntactic side, Uyghur has SOV constituent order, and considered a free-constituent order language. Uyghur is also a pro-drop language, as the subject can be elided if necessary, and recovered from the agreement markers on the verb.

We aim at building a dependency treebank to provide basic resources for future NLP researches. Morphological structure plays an important role in finding syntactic relations between words in Uyghur sentences. So all texts are morphologically analysed by Uyghur Morphological Analyser (UMA) software (M. Aili et al., 2012), There are 13 basic POS tags as shown in Table 1.

No	tags	POS	No	tags	POS
1	N	Noun	7	I	Imitative
2	A	Adjective	8	C	Conjunction
3	M	Numeral	9	T	Particle
4	Q	Quantifier	10	E	Exclamation
5	D	Adverb	11	V	Verb
6	P	Pronoun	12	R	Postposition
			13	Y	Punctuation

Table 1. Basic Post Tags in Uyghur Languages

There are 23 dependency relations scheme in UyDT as general as possible which are listed in Table 2.

No.	Label	Relations	No.	Label	Relations
1	ABL	Ablative Adjunct	13	OBJ	Object
2	ATT	Attributive Modifiers	14	POSS	Possessor
3	ADV	Adverbial Modifier	15	POST	Postpositions
4	APPOS	Apposition	16	QUOT	Quotation
5	AUX	Auxiliary Verb	17	ROOT	ROOT of Sentence
6	CLAS	Classifier	18	PRED	predicate
7	COLL	Collocation	19	SUBJ	Subject
8	CONJ	Conjunction	20	CL	Clause
9	COORD	Coordination	21	IND	Independent component
10	DAT	Dative Adjunct	22	COP	Copula
11	INST	Instrumental Adjuncts	23	COMP	Comparison
12	LOC	Locative Adjunct			

Table 2.   Dependency relation tags in Uyghur Dependency Treebank

3   mapping

3.1   mapping POS-tagset

The UD part-of-speech (POS) tagset is an extension of The Google Universal POS tagset (Petrov et al., 2012) and contains 17 POS tags, whereas, in UyDT, there are only 13 POS tags. Fortunately, we could map most of them to Universal POS tags (e.g. N$\rightarrow$ Noun, A$\rightarrow$ADJ).

However, only 10 POS tags in UyDT are mapped one by one to UD POS tags, six of the UD POS tags are not used, two tags in Uyghur POS tags are mapped to a same UD POS tag , as : (1) we didn't identify auxiliary verbs in Uyghur which is actually a verb and called auxiliary verb only when combining with other substantive word and indicating a grammatical meaning ; (2) In UyDT POS tagset, pronoun is also tagged as noun, as a result, PROPN in UD POS tags is also not used as well; (3) there are some discussion about DET, as there is not a tag called DET in Uyghur POS tagset, but some words have the meaning in a specific situation, which are numbers most of time. (4) Other three tags (SCONJ , SYM and X) are not used in UyDT. (5) According to the description of INTJ, two tags in

UyDT (exclamation and imitative) matched with it. We provide a mapping from the Uyghur POS tagset to the UD tagset in Table 3.

UD	UyDT tag	UyDT POS	UD	UyDT tag	UyDT POS
ADJ	A	Adjective	NUM	M	Numeral
ADV	D	Adverb	PART	T	Particle
ADP	R	Postposition	PRON	P	Pronoun
*	Q	Quantifier	PUNCT	Y	Punctuation
CONJ	C	Conjunction	VERB	V	Verb
INTJ	*E* / *I*	*Exclamation* / *Imitative*	NOUN	N	Noun
PROPN	*		X	*	
AUX	*		SYM	*	
SCONJ	*		DET	*	

Table 3: Mapping of the UyDT's POS tagset to the UD's POS tagset

3.2 mapping relations

UD defines a set of 40 broadly applicable dependency relations, further allowing language – specific subtypes of these to be defined to meet the needs of specific resources. However, there are only 23 types of dependent relations in UyDT. The conversion from UyDT dependency annotation to UD required not only relabelling types, but also changes to the tree structure, obviously, it isn't a straightforward mappings. We use three steps to finish the conversing: rule based automatic label mappings; structural changes; manual checking. The details are as follows:

3.2.1 rule based automatic label mapping

Most of the dependency relations which defined in UyDT are included in the UD, but isn't one by one mapping. After comparing the Uyghur treebank relation description with UD description, we mapped Uyghur DT dependent relations to UD as following table. The relation 'ATT', for instance, could map to 'acl, amod, det, nummod', which of them should be chosen is another problem. To tackle with this problem, we settled priority and some limited rules on them according to our corpus features to choose one of them.

Uyghur	Universal	Uyghur	Universal
ATT	acl, amod, det, nummod	ADV	advcl, advmod
CL	advcl, parataxis	APPOS	appos
AUX	aux	POST	case
CONJ	cc	QUOT	ccomp
COLL	compound, mwe, list, name, nummod, goeswith	COORD	conj
COP	cop, neg	PRED	nsubj
IND	discourse, parataxis, vocative	OBJ	dobj, nmod:cau
LOC	nmod	DAT	nmod
COMP	nmod:comp	POSS	nmod:poss, nmod:part, nmod:poss
LOC	nmod:tmod	SUBJ	nsubj
ROOT	punct		

Table 3 Mapping of the UyDT dependent relation to UD dependent relation

For example, the dependent relation 'OBJ' in UyDT could map to 'dobj, dobj:cau, nmod:cau' in UD, considering that the rate of using causative word is less than using non-causative word, we decided map all the dependent relation 'OBJ' to 'dobj'; the dependent relation 'ATT' in UyDT could map to 'acl, amod, det, nummod'. After adding some limitation on the dependent relation 'ATT', such as when the word is tagged 'NOUN', map it to 'amod', when it is tagged 'NUM' map it 'amod', and tagged 'PRON' map it to 'det'. After rule based mapping, most of the dependent relations are transformed correctly, certainly including some wrong labels as well. Then, we manually checked and corrected them.

3.2.2   structural changes

The UD syntactic annotation is based on the universal Stanford Dependencies (SD) scheme (de Marneffe et al., 2014). One of the key properties of these schemes is that they emphasizes direct relation between content words, treating function words as dependents of content words rather than as their heads. However, it is not all the case in UyDT. Some function words such as copula or auxiliary words were head of the predicative, for when a copula or auxiliary attaching a word, it would indicate a grammatical meaning as well as get certain morphological forms. For example: '*u hetni yezip* **boldi** (he had written the letter); *yezip* **bolghan** *hetni oqudi* (he read the letter which had been written)'. In these examples, the word with bold font, generated from one stem *bol*, has different morphological form in each sentences to combine these words around it. Though it is auxiliary verb, produce relation 'aux' and marked as the head of the relation in UyDT. It contrasts with UD and needs to make some structural changes. We done this changes with manually, for structural changes were not easily automated. The following structural changes were made manually:

- aux & cop

  In the UyDT, the auxiliary and copula are treated similarly to a verb, and can function as the root of a sentence. However, the UD scheme analyses copula constructions differently: the predicate is regarded as the head of the phrase, and the auxiliary or copula is its dependent, as labelled by the 'aux' or 'cop'. See Figure.1 (a) and (b) for comparison.

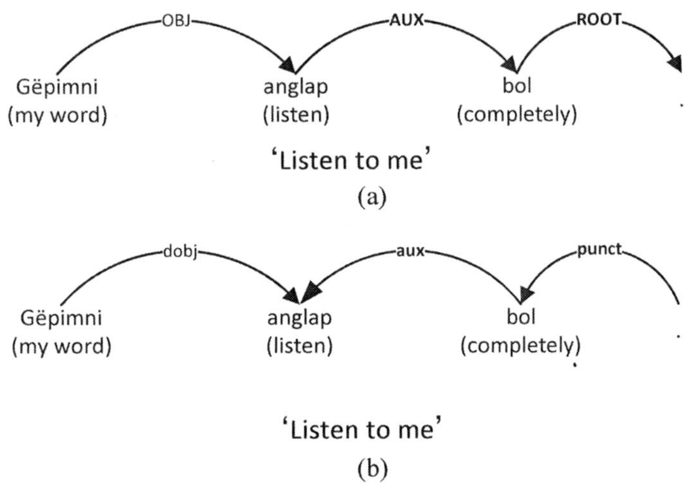

Figure 1: UD aux analysis

- punct

  In the UyDT, the punctuations which appeared in the sentence was not considered in dependent relation, instead, the last punctuation which appeared the end of a sentence was regarded as the head of the sentence and labelled as 'ROOT'. However, the UD defines a punctuation depend on content word which it always attached to with the relation of 'punct' and can never have dependents. It is need to change the relation structure and the label of the relation 'ROOT' in UyDT. (Figure 1)

- conj & cc

  Significant changes were made to the analysis of coordination. In the UyDT， defined words which formed coordinate relations depended from begin to end relatedly and the last one was the head of them with the label of 'COORD' . Meanwhile, the conjunction was depend on the coordinate word which it attached to with the label as 'CONJ' (Figure 2 (a)). The UD annotation scheme, on the other hand, uses right-adjunctions, where the first coordinate is the head of them, and the rest of phrase is adjoined to the right. We diverge from UD specification by marking the last conjunct as the head of the relation. All the other conjuncts depend on the last via labelling subsequent coordinates as 'conj' (Figure 2 (b))

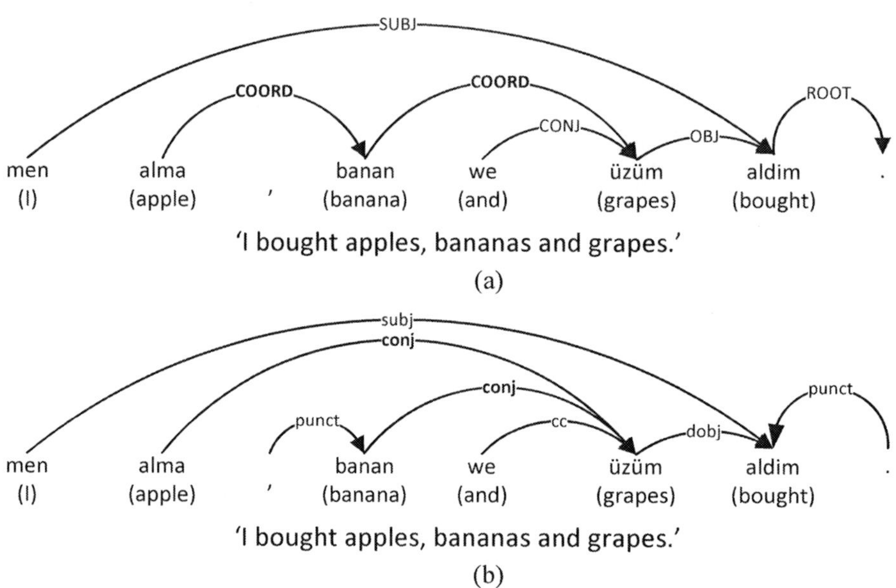

'I bought apples, bananas and grapes.'

(a)

'I bought apples, bananas and grapes.'

(b)

Figure 2: Coordination structure in the UD

3.2.3 Uyghur-specific relations

The UD scheme provides scope to include language-specific subtype labels. The label naming format is *unversal:extention,* which ensures that the core UD relation remains identifiable, making it possible to revert to this coarse label for cross-lingual analysis. During the conversion of the UyDT, we defined some labels required to represent Uyghur syntax more concisely. These labels are discussed below:

- advmod:emph
  Some adverbial modifiers in Uyghur has served as the emphasizer or intensifier. We use the subtype label 'advmod:emph' in cases where modifiers emphasize or intensify their heads. It is also used in the Turkish, Ancient Greek, Arabic, Czech, Latin, Portuguese and Tamil scheme as well. (Figure 3)

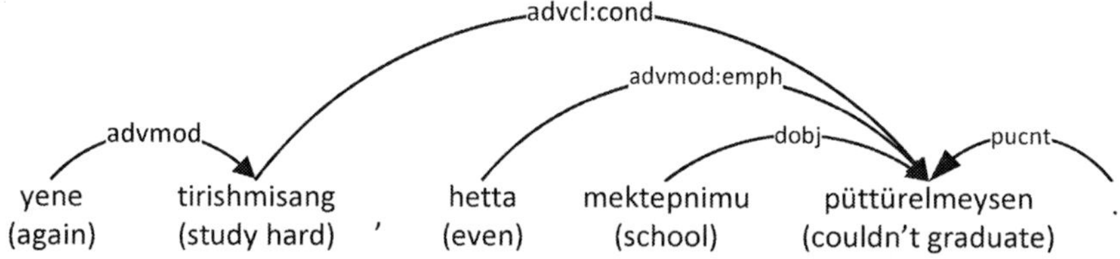

If you didn't study hard futher, you even couldn't graduate

Figure 3: UD advmod and advcl analysis

- advcl:cond
  It is used for conditional clauses. It is also used in Turkish scheme. (Figure 3)
- aux:q

In Uyghur, a question sentence is built by adding one of question particle to predicate (auxiliary verb or copula). We use 'aux:q' for all uses of the question particle. It also used in Hebrew, Turkish. (see Figure 4)

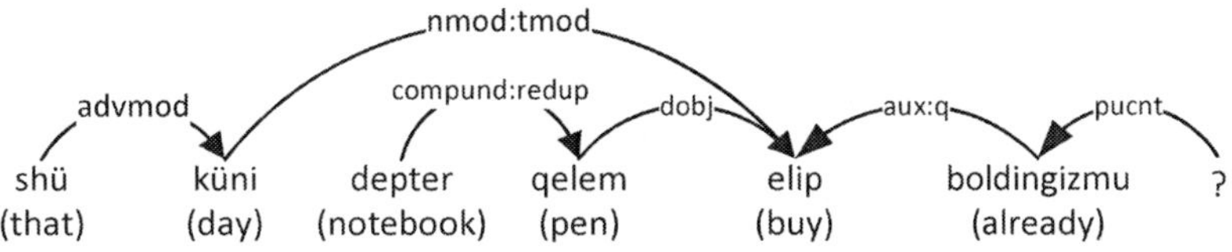

Figure 4: UD aux, compound and nmod analysis

- compound:redup
  Reduplication is a common process especially for adverbs, adjectives, nouns in Uyghur. Reduplication typically involves two identical words, but some morpho- phonological alternations are possible. The forms of the reduplicate words in Uyghur are various, this subtype of compound covers a range of reduplicated forms in Uyghur. It is also used in Turkish as well. An example is given in Figure 4.

- dobj:cau & nmod:cau
  We mark direct objects of causative verbs with 'dobj:cau', since the interpretation is different in comparison to a direct object of a non-causative verb. In general, if the verb is intransitive, direct object indicates the "causee", the subject of the content verb, or the entity that performs the action. If the verb is transitive, the direct object is the entity that is acted upon as in the non-causative case use the subtype 'nmod:cau' . They are also used in Turkish as well.

- nmod:tmod
  Temporal modifiers specifying time, in nominal form, are labelled as 'nmod:tmod'. English, Chinese, Danish, Russian etc. also uses this subtype label. See the Figure 4 for example.

- nmod:poss
  This subtype is used in possessive constructions, typically, the head of the construction is a possessive noun phrase, and the dependent is in genitive case. Danish, English, French, German, Kazakh etc. also use the subtype. An example is giben in Figure 5.

- nmod:comp
  This subtype of 'nmod' is used for marking comparative modifier of an adjective or adverb. The specific feature of it is a nominal word or phrase which attached ablative case suffix and an adjective or adverb. This subtype is also used in Turkish as well. See the Figure 5 for example.

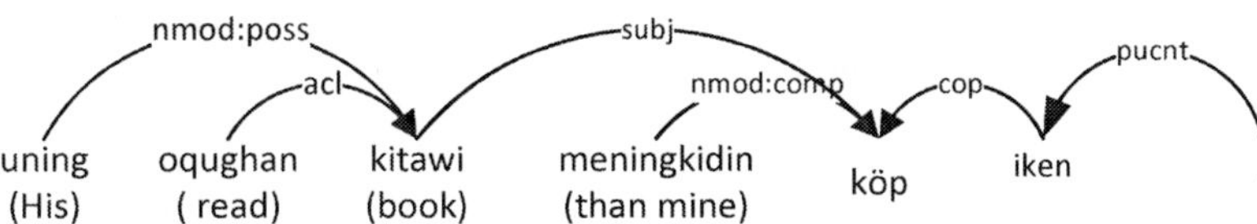

Figure 5: UD nmod relation analysis

- nmod:part
  This subtype of nmod is used for marking the part-whole relations. This structure is similar to 'nmod:poss' in most cases, but the range structures expressing "part of" is diverse, and distinction is often be useful.

4 summary and future work

In this paper, we have summarized the conversion of the Uyghur Dependency Treebank (UyDT) to UD format. We have described in detail the mapping and conversion process, including structural changes required, for the release of the UyDT as part of the Universal Dependencies project. We have also discussed linguistic analyses and motivations for choosing of Uyghur language-specific label types.

Acknowledgments

This work was funded by the Natural Science Foundation of China (Grant No. 61262061) and supported by Science & Technology Foundation of Xinjiang(Grant No. 201423120).
We are extremely thankful to the mathematical and physical department in Charles University and in particular to Dan Zeman for his advice on the Uyghur conversion effort.

Reference

Aili, M., Xialifu, A., Maihefureti, & Maimaitimin, S. (2016). Building Uyghur Dependency Treebank: Design Principles, Annotation Schema and Tools. In Lecture Notes in Computer Science (including subseries Lecture Notes in Artificial Intelligence and Lecture Notes in Bioinformatics) (Vol. 9442, pp. 124–136).

de Marneffe, M.-C., Dozat, T., Silveira, N., Haverinen, K., Ginter, F., Nivre, J., & Manning, C. D. (2014). Universal Stanford Dependencies: A cross-linguistic typology. In Proceedings of the Ninth International Conference on Language Resources and Evaluation (LREC'14), 4585–4592.

Džeroski, S., Erjavec, T., & Ledinek, N. (2006). Towards a Slovene dependency treebank. Proc. of the Fifth Intern. …, (May), 1388–1391.

Hajičová, E. (1998). Prague Dependency Treebank: From Analytic to Tectogrammatical Annotation. In Proceedings of the First Workshop on Text, Speech, Dialogue (pp. 45–50).

Haverinen, K., Viljanen, T., Laippala, V., Kohonen, S., Ginter, F., & Salakoski, T. (2010). Treebanking Finnish. In In proc. of The Ninth International Workshop on Treebanks and Linguistic Treories (TLT-9) (pp. 79–90).

Kromann, M. T. (2003). The Danish Dependency Treebank and the DTAG Treebank Tool. In Proceedings of the Second Workshop on Treebanks and Linguistic Theories (pp. 217–220).

Lynn, T., & Foster, J. (2016). Universal dependencies for Irish. In Celtic Language Technology Workshop (pp. 79–92).

Mairehaba·, A., Jiang, W., Wang, Z., Tuergen·, Y., & Liu, Q. (2012). Directed Graph Model of Uyghur Morphological Analysis. Journal of Software, 23(12), 3115–3129.

Mamitimin, S., Ibrahim, T., & Eli, M. (2013). The Annotation Scheme for Uyghur Dependency Treebank. 2013 International Conference on Asian Language Processing, 185–188.

Mcdonald, R., Nivre, J., Quirmbach-brundage, Y., Goldberg, Y., Das, D., Ganchev, K., … Lee, J. (2013). Universal Dependency Annotation for Multilingual Parsing. Proceedings of the 51st Annual Meeting of the Association for Computational Linguistics, 92–97.

McDonald, R., Petrov, S., & Hall, K. (2011). Multi-source transfer of delexicalized dependency parsers. Proceedings of the Conference on Empirical Methods in Natural Language Processing, (2007), 62–72.

Oflazer, K. (2003). BUILDING A TURKISH TREEBANK, 1–17.

Petrov, S., Das, D., & Mcdonald, R. (2012). A Universal Part-of-Speech Tagset. Proceedings of the Eighth International Conference on Language Resources and Evaluation (LREC '12), 2089–2096.

Pyysalo, S., Kanerva, J., Missilä, A., Laippala, V., & Ginter, F. (2015). Universal Dependencies for Finnish. Nordic Conference of Computational Linguistics NODALIDA 2015, (Nodalida), 163.

Søgaard, A. (2011). Data Point Selection for Cross-Language Adaptation of Dependency Parsers. Proceedings of the 49th Annual Meeting of the Association for Computational Linguistics: Human Language Technologies (HLT '11): Short Papers, 682–686.

Tsarfaty, R. (2013). A Unified Morpho-Syntactic Scheme of Stanford Dependencies. Proceedings of the 51st Annual Meeting of the Association for Computational Linguistics (Volume 2: Short Papers), 578–584.

Zeman, D. (2008). Reusable Tagset Conversion Using Tagset Drivers. Lrec, 213–218.

A non-expert Kaldi recipe for Vietnamese Speech Recognition System

Hieu-Thi Luong
VNUHCM - University of Science
Ho Chi Minh City, Vietnam
luonghieuthi@gmail.com

Hai-Quan Vu
VNUHCM - University of Science
Ho Chi Minh City, Vietnam
vhquan@fit.hcmus.edu.vn

Abstract

In this paper we describe a non-expert setup for Vietnamese speech recognition system using Kaldi toolkit. We collected a speech corpus over fifteen hours from about fifty Vietnamese native speakers and using it to test the feasibility of our setup. The essential linguistic components for the Automatic Speech Recognition (ASR) system was prepared basing on the written form of the language instead of expertise knowledge on linguistic and phonology as commonly seen in rich resource languages like English. The modeling of tones by integrating them into the phoneme and using the phonetic decision tree is also discussed. Experimental results showed this setup for ASR systems does yield competitive results while have potentials for further improvements.

1 Introduction

Thanks to the improvement by applying deep learning for speech recognition systems (Dahl et al., 2012; Hinton et al., 2012), speech recognition has gained more attention from both research and industrial community. However for minority languages such as Vietnamese, the number of research groups and publications are still limited. One reason for this is the lack of available resources concern of speech recognition and linguistic in general. There are a few attempts to enrich the resources for such languages. One notable example is the GlobalPhone database (Schultz et al., 2013; Schultz and Schlippe, 2014), which provide speech, text data as well as the pronunciation dictionary based on International Phonetic Alphabet (IPA) (International Phonetic Association, 1999) for 20 languages, Vietnamese included. Although for independent researchers it's not feasible to access these public dataset as the cost is quite expensive.

Kaldi (Povey et al., 2011) is an open source Speech Recognition Toolkit and quite popular among the research community. Thanks to the active development, Kaldi is regularly updated with new implementation of state-of-the-art techniques and recipes for speech recognition systems. One motivation for us to define a Vietnamese recipe is to take advantages of such available resources. Another reason is to establish a simple and straightforward Vietnamese recipe so more researchers can start to work on speech recognition system for Vietnamese. In the remain of this paper, Section 2 describes the data we used for the experiments. Section 3 shows the approach for preparing essential linguistic components and describe unique characteristics of Vietnamese languages. Section 4 explains the acoustic modeling and the techniques used to improve the performance of the ASR system. Section 5 evaluates all described recipes while Sections 6 gives a conclusion for our work.

2 Data preparation

2.1 Speech corpus

To evaluate our recipe we prepared a speech corpus by recording speech data from more than 50 native Vietnamese volunteers. For training, 46 speakers (22 males and 24 females) help record 15 hours of speech with 11660 utterances in total. While for testing another set of 19 speakers (12 males and 7

Proceedings of WLSI/OIAF4HLT,
pages 51–55, Osaka, Japan, December 12 2016.

females) recorded 50 minutes of speech with 760 utterances in totals. The recording sessions were conducted in a quiet environment using quality equipments. The size of the corpus is quite small for the current standard of ASR system, however similar size corpus have been commonly used to evaluate Vietnamese ASR system (Quang et al., 2008; Le and Besacier, 2009). We refer to the corpus as VIVOS, more details about the corpus can be found at `http://ailab.hcmus.edu.vn/vivos`.

Table 1: Speech corpus statistics

Set	Speakers	Male	Female	Utterances	Duration	Unique Syllables
Traing	46	22	24	11660	14:55	4617
Testing	19	12	7	760	00:45	1692

2.2 Text corpus

Language model is still an essential part of any state-of-the-art ASR system. In our experiment about 500 MB of text collected from online news and forum from the last 5 years was used to train the decoding language model. The text was first normalized to remove symbols, tags or other non-language elements. Popular abbreviation and numeric expression then replaced by their unrolled written form. The remain text still contained a lot of foreign or incorrect words but was keep as it is and handled in later stage.

3 Linguistic components

3.1 Syllable-based Language Model

In the writing system of Vietnamese language, spaces are used to separated syllables instead of words as in English. Some other languages that share similar trait are Chinese and Japanese. To follow the conventional definition of word in an ASR system one extra step known as word segmentation need to be taken. A Vietnamese word can contain from one up to four syllables, the boundary between words then need to be determined in the segmentation step. Word segmentation is not a trivial task and there is no perfect technique to solve this problem.

For simplification a syllable-based language model can be used instead of word-based. Syllable-based language model helps avoid errors caused by segmentation step and reduce the complexity as the number of syllables is fewer. In our work a trigram syllable-based language model was trained using the text corpus described in previous section. The vocabulary contains 7746 most used Vietnamese-only syllables and the language model was processed to only contain these syllables. As Kaldi would map words and phonemes to their respective integer id, this allows all Vietnamese text to be kept in their Unicode encoding.

3.2 Grapheme-based Pronunciation Dictionary

For Vietnamese ASR systemsm there isn't an standard dominant pronunciation dictionary. In the GlobalPhone database, IPA was used to construct pronunciation dictionaries for all languages. This unified phoneset open the possibility for multi-language speech recognition system. Although it would be harder to model the unique characteristics of each languages. Another approach is following the Vietnamese phonology definition which suggested that each syllables consist of five components with some components can be redundant. This approach creates a bigger phoneset as it contains diphthong and triphthong. Another approach is using grapheme as phoneme with each character considered as a phoneme as done by Le and Besacier (2009).

In this paper we propose a grapheme-based pronunciation dictionary but not strictly mapping from one character to one phoneme. To simplify the recipe the role and position of each component in syllable is ignored and only two type of phonemes are defined: consonants and vowels. A consonant can be one or up to three characters (instead of one character as grapheme phoneset) while a vowel is a standard vowel with a respective tone. In this setup each tonal variations of a vowel is treated as different phonemes with no relation. To regain tonal information, extra questions could be used to build the phonetic decision tree, the details of this tonal modeling would be discussed in Sections 4.3.

52

Table 2: Tone integrated grapheme-based phoneset with 99 phonemes in total

Consonants	3 characters	ngh
	2 characters	ch gh gi kh ng nh ph qu tr th
	1 character	b c d đ g h k l m n p r s t v
Vowels	[blank]	a ă â e ê i o ô ơ u ư y
	grave accent	á ắ ấ é ế í ó ố ớ ú ứ ý
	acute accent	à ằ ầ è ề ì ò ồ ờ ù ừ ỳ
	hook	ả ẳ ẩ ẻ ể ỉ ỏ ổ ở ủ ử ỷ
	tilde	ã ẵ ẫ ẽ ễ ĩ õ ỗ ỡ ũ ữ ỹ
	dot below	ạ ặ ậ ẹ ệ ị ọ ộ ợ ụ ự y

It's a well known fact that [ngh] and [ng] is two written form of the same phoneme in Vietnamese. But to keep our setup grapheme-based and easy to follow even for people who do not speak the language, we decided to not combine them and leave such enhancements and other exceptions for future works.

Table 3: Example entries for grapheme-based pronunciation dictionary

nhanh nh a nh	chào ch à o	tôi t ô i
nghiêng ngh i ê ng	ba b a	tối t ố i

4 Systems description

4.1 Acoustic modeling

For acoustic modeling we followed standard recipes of Kaldi. The acoustic features used is 13 dimensions Mel-Frequency Cepstral Coeffiennts (MFCC) with Linear Discriminative Analysis (LDA) and Maximum Likelihood Linear Transform (MLLT) applied to 7-splice (3 left and 3 right context) frames and project to a 40-dimensions feature. This feature used to train a conventional triphone GMM acoustic model. Next a discriminative training method Maximum Mutual Information (MMI) was used to train the second model (Povey et al., 2008). A speaker dependent model then trained by applying feature-based Maximum Likelihood Linear Regression (fMLLR) to the acoustic feature (Povey and Saon, 2006). The last model is a hybrid HMM-DNN where DNN was trained to classification the input feature to the corresponding HMM tied states, the fMLLR transformed feature are used to train the hybrid model.

For summary, we trained 4 models: a triphone GMM-based baseline (mGMM), one discriminative trained (mGMM+MMI), one speaker adaptation for GMM (mGMM+SAT) and a hybrid HMM-DNN model with speaker adapted feature (mDNN+SAT). All GMM models contains about 15000 gaussians and 2500 leaves. As for HMM-DNN hybrid setup, DNN contains only 2 hidden layers each with just 300 nodes. The parameters was small when comparing with other Kaldi recipes as the data available for our training is limited.

4.2 Pitch feature for tonal languages

Ghahremani et al. (2014) showed that pitch feature can be helpful for ASR systems especially for tonal languages like Vietnamese and Cantonese. Their implementation for pitch feature extraction is distributed with Kaldi framework. To investigate the effectiveness of pitch in our setup another set of 4 models described above are trained with just one different: pitch feature was augmented into the acoustic features before applied LDA and MLLT.

4.3 Tones clustering using Phonetic Decision Trees

There are some study about modeling tonal information to improve the accuracy of Vietnamses ASR system (Vu and Schultz, 2010; Nguyen et al., 2015) although they are all fall into one of these two approaches: tones are considered as separate phonemes (explicit tone model), or tones are integrated into a phoneme and creating 6 different variation of the same base phoneme (data-driven tone model).

As described in Section 3.2 a tone integrated phoneset is used for our recipes and without further customization our setup is similar to the data-driven tone model (with a slightly different phoneset). To help recreate the relations between the tonal variations of the same base phoneme we utilized the extra questions used to build the phonetic decision tree (Young et al., 1994) to let it asks about tonal questions. This way we can create a more sophisticated modeling for tones and it's also a novel part in our work.

For a typical Kaldi recipe, the question used to build the decision tree are generated automatic based on the tree-clustering of the phones (Povey et al., 2011). Thanks to the flexible structure of Kaldi framework, extra questions about linguistic knowledge can be supplied to further tuning for a particular language. As for Vietnamese we added two simple set of questions about tones: question to group phonemes with same base vowel together and question to group phonemes with the same tone together.

Table 4: Examples of extra questions used to incorporate tones into the decision tree

Same base vowel	Same tone
a á à ả ã ạ	a ă â e ê i o ô ơ u ư y
ă ắ ằ ẳ ẵ ặ	á ắ ấ é ế í ó ố ớ ú ứ ý

5 Evaluations

Three different recipes followed the description in Section 4 were prepared and evaluated, each with 4 models: the baseline setup using the grapheme-based pronunciation dictionary and standard MFCC feature (baseline), the second recipe with the augmenting of pitch into the acoustic feature (+pitch) and the last one with pitch feature and the incorporation of tones to the phonetic decision tree (+tone).

Table 5: %SyER for 3 recipe each with 4 different models

	baseline	+pitch	+tones
mGMM	19.66	15.14	14.91
mGMM+MMI	18.08	14.96	13.91
mGMM+SAT	15.79	12.07	12.13
mDNN+SAT	13.34	9.54	9.48

Table 5 showed the Syllable Error Rate (%SyER) of three recipes described above. The baseline recipe has a 19.66%SyER for mGMM model and gain 1.58% absolute improvement when training using discriminative method. The mGMM+SAT model trained with the speaker adaptation method fMLLR achieved the best result in all three GMM-based models. While the hybrid HMM-DNN system trained with adapted featured further improve the performance to 13.34 %SyER. This result confirmed the validity of our non-expert recipe for Vietnamese ASR system.

The second recipe with the addition of pitch feature greatly improve the performance in all 4 models. The lowest error is 9.54 %SyER achieved using mDNN+SAT. This once again shows the benefit of using pitch for Vietnamese system. The last recipe with pitch and the incorporation of tones to the decision tree slightly improve the results in the conventional mGMM model and a notable improvement (1% absolute) in mGMM-MMI. However the improvement fades away with 2 models using speaker adaptation technique. This showed the potential of using extra questions for more sophisticated modeling of tones or other linguistic characteristic of Vietnamese.

6 Conclusions

In this work we prepared a toy Vietnamese speech corpus suitable for testing a new speech recognition setup. A grapheme-based Kaldi recipe was established using common information about the language instead of expert knowledge. The tonal information are incorporated into the phonetic decision tree and also show promising result. Similar setups can be constructed for other languages and even if the results do not surpass their counterpart phonetic approach, the using of grapheme-based approach can be useful for tasks like multi-lingual or cross-lingual speech recognition and speech synthesis.

References

George E Dahl, Dong Yu, Li Deng, and Alex Acero. 2012. Context-dependent pre-trained deep neural networks for large-vocabulary speech recognition. *IEEE Transactions on Audio, Speech, and Language Processing*, 20(1):30–42.

Pegah Ghahremani, Bagher BabaAli, Daniel Povey, Korbinian Riedhammer, Jan Trmal, and Sanjeev Khudanpur. 2014. A pitch extraction algorithm tuned for automatic speech recognition. In *Proc. ICASSP*, pages 2494–2498. IEEE.

Geoffrey Hinton, Li Deng, Dong Yu, George E Dahl, Abdel-rahman Mohamed, Navdeep Jaitly, Andrew Senior, Vincent Vanhoucke, Patrick Nguyen, Tara N Sainath, and Brian Kingsbury. 2012. Deep neural networks for acoustic modeling in speech recognition: The shared views of four research groups. *IEEE Signal Processing Magazine*, 29(6):82–97.

International Phonetic Association. 1999. *Handbook of the International Phonetic Association: A guide to the use of the International Phonetic Alphabet.* Cambridge University Press.

Viet-Bac Le and Laurent Besacier. 2009. Automatic speech recognition for under-resourced languages: application to Vietnamese language. *IEEE Transactions on Audio, Speech, and Language Processing*, 17:1471–1482.

Thien Chuong Nguyen, Josef Chaloupka, and Jan Nouza. 2015. Study on incorporating tone into speech recognition of Vietnamese. In *Proc. ECMSM*, pages 1–6. IEEE.

Daniel Povey and George Saon. 2006. Feature and model space speaker adaptation with full covariance Gaussians. In *Proc. Interspeech*.

Daniel Povey, Dimitri Kanevsky, Brian Kingsbury, Bhuvana Ramabhadran, George Saon, and Karthik Visweswariah. 2008. Boosted MMI for model and feature-space discriminative training. In *2008 IEEE International Conference on Acoustics, Speech and Signal Processing*, pages 4057–4060. IEEE.

Daniel Povey, Arnab Ghoshal, Gilles Boulianne, Lukas Burget, Ondrej Glembek, Nagendra Goel, Mirko Hannemann, Petr Motlicek, Yanmin Qian, Petr Schwarz, Jan Silovský, Georg Stemmer, and Karel Veselý. 2011. The Kaldi speech recognition toolkit. In *Proc. IEEE ASRU*. IEEE Signal Processing Society.

Nguyen Hong Quang, Pascal Nocera, Eric Castelli, and Trinh Van Loan. 2008. A novel approach in continuous speech recognition for Vietnamese, an isolating tonal language. *Proc. SLTU*.

Tanja Schultz and Tim Schlippe. 2014. Globalphone: Pronunciation dictionaries in 20 languages. In *Proc. LREC*, pages 337–341.

Tanja Schultz, Ngoc Thang Vu, and Tim Schlippe. 2013. Globalphone: A multilingual text & speech database in 20 languages. In *Proc. ICASSP*, pages 8126–8130. IEEE.

Ngoc Thang Vu and Tanja Schultz. 2010. Optimization on Vietnamese large vocabulary speech recognition. In *Proc. SLTU*, pages 104–110.

Steve J Young, Julian J Odell, and Philip C Woodland. 1994. Tree-based state tying for high accuracy acoustic modelling. In *Proc. ARPA Human Language Technology Workshop*, pages 307–312. Association for Computational Linguistics.

Evaluating Ensemble Based Pre-annotation on Named Entity Corpus Construction in English and Chinese

Tingming Lu[1,2], Man Zhu[3], Zhiqiang Gao[1,2], and Yaocheng Gui[1,2]
[1]Key Lab of Computer Network and Information Integration (Southeast University),
Ministry of Education, China
[2]School of Computer Science and Engineering, Southeast University, China
[3]School of Computer Science and Technology,
Nanjing University of Posts and Telecommunications, China
`lutingming@163.com,mzhu@njupt.edu.cn,{zqgao,yaochgui}@seu.edu.cn`

Abstract

Annotated corpora are crucial language resources, and pre-annotation is an usual way to reduce the cost of corpus construction. Ensemble based pre-annotation approach combines multiple existing named entity taggers and categorizes annotations into *normal annotations* with high confidence and *candidate annotations* with low confidence, to reduce the human annotation time. In this paper, we manually annotate three English datasets under various pre-annotation conditions, report the effects of ensemble based pre-annotation, and analyze the experimental results. In order to verify the effectiveness of ensemble based pre-annotation in other languages, such as Chinese, three Chinese datasets are also tested. The experimental results show that the ensemble based pre-annotation approach significantly reduces the number of annotations which human annotators have to add, and outperforms the baseline approaches in reduction of human annotation time without loss in annotation performance (in terms of F_1-measure), on both English and Chinese datasets.

1 Introduction

The current success and widespread use of machine learning techniques for processing human language make annotated corpora essential language resources. Many popular natural language processing (NLP) algorithms require large amounts of high-quality training samples, which are time-consuming and costly to build. One usual way to improve this situation is to automatically pre-annotate the corpora, so that human annotators need merely to correct errors rather than to annotate from scratch.

Named Entity Recognition (NER), one of the fundamental tasks for building NLP systems, is a task that detects Named Entity (NE) mentions in a given text and classifies these mentions to a predefined list of types. Resulted from more than two decades of research, many named entity taggers are publicly available now. Some of the taggers are integrated into NLP workflows based on Service Oriented Architecture (Ide et al., 2015; Piperidis et al., 2015). And it is well known that multiple taggers can be combined using ensemble techniques to create a system that outperforms the best individual tagger within the system (Wu et al., 2003; Speck and Ngomo, 2014). However, only a few studies have been reported on leveraging ensemble to combine multiple existing taggers to assist named entity annotation.

Lu et al. (2016) introduced ensemble based pre-annotation approach in named entity corpus construction. They conducted experiments on an English dataset, and the results showed that the ensemble based pre-annotation approach outperforms the baseline approaches in reduction of human annotation time.

In this paper, we perform a more thorough evaluation on the ensemble based pre-annotation approach. 1) We manually annotate three English datasets under various pre-annotation conditions, report the effects of ensemble based pre-annotation, and analyze the experimental results. 2) We also manually annotate three Chinese datasets, to verify the effectiveness of ensemble based pre-annotation in Chinese language.

The remaining part of this paper is organized as follows: In Section 2, we mention related work. Section 3 describes the experimental setup, followed by experimental results and analysis in Section 4. Finally, we conclude and discuss future directions in Section 5.

Proceedings of WLSI/OIAF4HLT,
pages 56–60, Osaka, Japan, December 12 2016.

2   Related Work

Given the importance of annotated corpora to NLP system development, many applications for different domains have been built in order to assist named entity annotation, using a single tagger (Lingren et al., 2014; Ogren et al., 2008), or multiple taggers (Ganchev et al., 2007).

The goal of an ensemble learning algorithm is to generate a classifier with a high predictive performance by combining the predictions of a set of basic classifiers. Previous work has already suggested that ensemble learning can be used to improve NER (Wu et al., 2003; Speck and Ngomo, 2014; Florian et al., 2003; Desmet and Hoste, 2010). Speck and Ngomo (2014) combined four state-of-the-art taggers by using 15 different algorithms for ensemble learning and evaluated their performance on five datasets. Their results suggested that ensemble learning can reduce the error rate of state-of-the-art NER systems by 40%.

We follow Lu et al. (2016) and perform a more thorough evaluation on the ensemble based pre-annotation. We manually annotate three English datasets and three Chinese datasets, report the performance, and analyze the results.

3   Experimental Setup

3.1   Datasets

All the datasets used in our experiments are publicly available. There are three English datasets, and three Chinese datasets. From each dataset, 60 articles are selected randomly. From each of the 60 articles, one sentence is extracted to perform the actual assisted annotation experiments. Sentences containing more NEs are preferred over ones containing less NEs. Sentences containing no NE will not be extracted. The three English datasets have been described in Lu et al. (2016). The three Chinese datasets are People's Daily (Fu and Luke, 2005), Penn Chinese Treebank 5.1 (CTB5) (Xue et al., 2005), and ITNLP[1].

3.2   Taggers

Six English NE taggers and three Chinese NE taggers are involved in our experiments. They are all public available. For outputs of these taggers, only three types are considered in our experiments, namely Person, Location, and Organization. The English NE taggers are the same as the ones described in Lu et al. (2016). The Chinese NE taggers are ICTCLAS[2] (Liu et al., 2004), FudanNLP[3] (Qiu et al., 2013) and Stanford Named Entity Recognizer[4] (Stanford(zh))(Manning et al., 2014).

3.3   Pre-annotators

For the English taggers, the pre-annotator Ensemble(en) which combines six taggers and produces *normal* and *candidate annotations* is used to evaluate the ensemble based pre-annotation approach. One baseline pre-annotator using a single tagger is denoted as Stanford(en). Another baseline pre-annotator Stanford(en)+Illinois produces annotations which are union of the outputs of two taggers, namely Stanford(en) and Illinois. No ensemble technique is applied on the pre-annotator Stanford(en) and Illinois. We choose Stanford(en) and Illinois because they are the best two taggers in terms of F_1-measure on the test datasets.

Similarly, for the Chinese taggers, the pre-annotator Ensemble(zh) combines three taggers. One baseline pre-annotator using a single tagger is ICTCLAS. Another baseline pre-annotator ICTCLAS+Stanford(zh) produces annotations which are union of the outputs of the two taggers.

For the ensemble based pre-annotators (Ensemble(en) and Ensemble(zh)), Weighted Voting (Zhou, 2012) is used to weight the different taggers. The ensemble based pre-annotators learn the weights incrementally after each sentence in a dataset is annotated by human.

---

[1] http://www.datatang.com/data/44067/
[2] http://ictclas.nlpir.org/ (version 5.0).
[3] http://nlp.fudan.edu.cn/ (version 2.1).
[4] http://nlp.stanford.edu/software/CRF-NER.shtml (version 3.6.0).

Table 1: Assisted annotation experiments. Annotators are assigned to annotate sentences under various pre-annotation conditions.

Dataset	H$_1$	H$_2$	H$_3$
AKSW-News	Stanford(en)	Ensemble(en)	Stanford(en)+Illinois
CoNLL-Test	Stanford(en)+Illinois	Stanford(en)	Ensemble(en)
Reuters-128	Ensemble(en)	Stanford(en)+Illinois	Stanford(en)
CTB5	ICTCLAS	Ensemble(zh)	ICTCLAS+Stanford(zh)
ITNLP	ICTCLAS+Stanford(zh)	ICTCLAS	Ensemble(zh)
People's Daily	Ensemble(zh)	ICTCLAS+Stanford(zh)	ICTCLAS

Table 2: Results of assisted annotation experiments.

Pre-annotator	Language	N_{add}	N_{modify}	Precision	Recall	F$_1$	Time
Stanford(en)	English	0.47	**0.16**	0.947	0.923	0.935	18.8
Stanford(en)+Illinois	English	0.37	0.46	0.942	0.924	0.933	18.7
Ensemble(en)	English	**0.11**	0.67	0.950	0.930	0.940	**18.2**
ICTCLAS	Chinese	1.32	**0.08**	0.948	0.936	0.942	14.6
ICTCLAS+Stanford(zh)	Chinese	0.82	0.91	0.949	0.947	0.948	14.6
Ensemble(zh)	Chinese	**0.59**	0.84	0.951	0.951	0.951	**13.3**

3.4 Assisted Annotation Experiments

Three human annotators (H$_1$, H$_2$, and H$_3$) participate in our assisted annotation experiments. They are graduate students in our school, and major in NLP study. After they have annotated some sentences in a training dataset to get familiar with the Web based UI, each of them has to annotate all of the sentences in the six datasets. The human annotators are presented with the sentences in the same order (Table 1), but for different human annotators, each sentence is pre-annotated by different pre-annotators. We carefully design the experiments, to ensure that each sentence will be pre-annotated by all the pre-annotators, and will be annotated by all the human annotators.

4 Results and Analysis

The results of assisted annotation experiments under various pre-annotation conditions are presented in Table 2. After the sentences are pre-annotated by ensemble based pre-annotators (Ensemble(en) and Ensemble(zh)), human annotators take less annotation time per sentence without loss in annotation performance (in terms of F$_1$-measure), on both English and Chinese datasets.

The Web based UI automaticly records the number of *adding actions* (N_{add}) and number of *modifying actions* (N_{modify}) when human annotators are annotating. As presented in Table 2, ensemble based pre-annotation approach significantly reduces the number of *adding actions*. However, ensemble based pre-annotation approach introduces more *modifying actions*, compared to single taggers (Stanford(en) and ICTCLAS). We will analyze the results in the following.

We utilize linear regression to model the annotation time, where T_{total} is the total time in seconds spent on a sentence, N_{token} is the number of English tokens or Chinese characters in the sentence, T_{token} is the time taken on reading an English token or a Chinese character, N_{add} is the number of *adding actions*, T_{add} is the time taken on performing an *adding action*, N_{modify} is the number of *modifying actions*, T_{modify} is the time taken on performing a *modifying action*, and additionally, there is T_c seconds of overhead per sentence.

$$T_{Total} = N_{token} \cdot T_{token} + N_{add} \cdot T_{add} + N_{modify} \cdot T_{modify} + T_c$$

Table 3: Estimated time spent on reading a token, adding a new annotation, modifying an existed annotation, etc.

Language	T_{token}	T_{add}	T_{modify}	T_c
English	0.25	4.79	1.95	7.45
Chinese	0.11	4.22	1.94	1.64

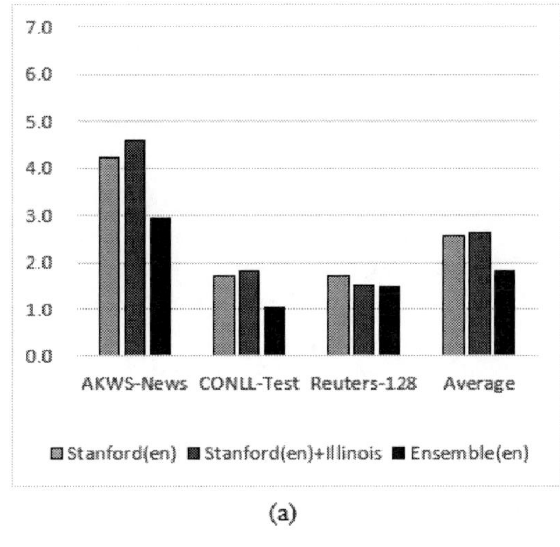

(a)

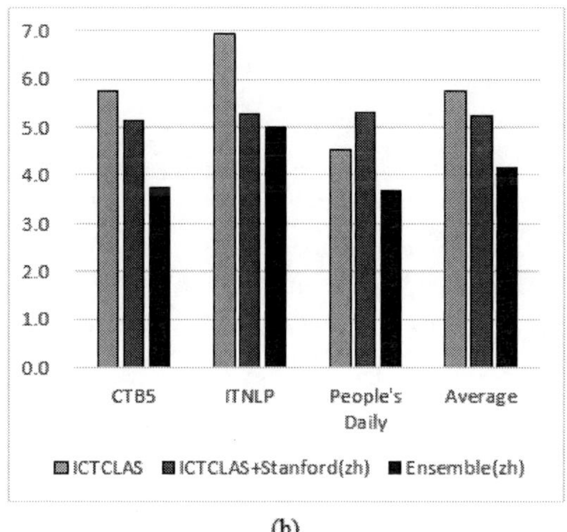

(b)

Figure 1: Estimated time taken by human annotators on performing adding and modifying actions on English (a) and Chinese (b) datasets.

There are 180 sentences in the three English datasets. Each of them is pre-annotated by three pre-annotators, and then annotated by three human annotators. Finally we get 540 instances. Similarly, from the experimental results on the Chinese datasets, we get 540 instances. Based on the time model, we get T_{token}, T_{add}, T_{modify}, and T_c, as listed in Table 3. As we can see, adding a new annotation takes twice more time than modifying an existing annotation, both on English and Chinese datasets.

Given a sentence under different pre-annotation conditions, $N_{token} \cdot T_{token} + T_c$ is constant, while the *adding* and *modifying action* time $T_{a+m} = N_{add} \cdot T_{add} + N_{modify} \cdot T_{modify}$ varies. Now, we can estimate the *adding* and *modifying action* time for the different pre-annotation approaches on all the datasets. From Figure 1, we can see that after the sentences are pre-annotated by ensemble based pre-annotators, human annotators take less time on performing *adding* and *modifying actions* than the two baseline approaches on all datasets.

5   Conclusion

In this paper, we evaluate the effects of ensemble based pre-annotation which combines multiple existing NE taggers on three English datasets and three Chinese datasets. The experimental results show that the ensemble based pre-annotation approach reduces the number of *adding actions* and the total human annotation time, without loss in annotation performance (in terms of F_1-measure). Based on a linear regression model, we estimate the time taken on performing *adding* and *modifying actions* by human annotators, and conclude that ensemble based pre-annotation approach reduces the human annotation time on all datasets. In future work, we will study how different ensemble algorithms affect the performance, and will try to apply ensemble based pre-annotation approach to other NLP tasks, such as Entity Linking, Relation Extraction, etc.

Acknowledgements

This work is partially funded by the National Science Foundation of China under Grant 61170165, 61602260, 61502095. We would like to thank all the anonymous reviewers for their helpful comments.

References

Bart Desmet, and Vronique Hoste 2010. Dutch named entity recognition using classifier ensembles. *LOT Occasional Series*, vol 16, pp. 29–41.

Radu Florian, Abe Ittycheriah, Hongyan Jing, and Tong Zhang. 2003. Named entity recognition through classifier combination. *Proceedings of the Seventh Conference on Natural Language Learning at HLT-NAACL*, vol 4. Association for Computational Linguistics.

Guohong Fu, and Kang-Kwong Luke. 2005. Chinese named entity recognition using lexicalized HMMs. *ACM SIGKDD Explorations Newsletter*, vol. 7, no. 1, pp.19–25.

Kuzman Ganchev, Fernando Pereira, and Mark Mandel. 2007. Semi-automated named entity annotation. *Proceedings of the linguistic annotation workshop,* pp. 53–56. Association for Computational Linguistics.

Nancy Ide, James Pustejovsky, Christopher Cieri, Eric Nyberg, Denise DiPersio, Chunqi Shi, Keith Suderman, Marc Verhagen, Di Wang, and Jonathan Wright. 2015. The language application grid. *International Workshop on Worldwide Language Service Infrastructure*, (pp. 51–70). Springer International Publishing.

Todd Lingren, Louise Deleger, Katalin Molnar, Haijun Zhai, Jareen Meinzen-Derr, Megan Kaiser, Laura Stoutenborough, Qi Li, and Imre Solti. 2014. Evaluating the impact of pre-annotation on annotation speed and potential bias: natural language processing gold standard development for clinical named entity recognition in clinical trial announcements. *Journal of the American Medical Informatics Association,* 21(3), 406-413.

Qun Liu, Huaping Zhang, Hongkui Yu, and Xueqi Cheng. 2004. Chinese lexical analysis using cascaded hidden Markov model. *Journal of Computer Research and Development*, vol. 41, no. 8, pp. 1421–1429.

Tingming Lu, Man Zhu, and Zhiqiang Gao. (under publication) 2016. Reducing Human Effort in Named Entity Corpus Construction Based on Ensemble Learning and Annotation Categorization.

Christopher D. Manning, Mihai Surdeanu, John Bauer, Jenny Finkel, Steven J. Bethard, and David McClosky. 2014. The Stanford CoreNLP Natural Language Processing Toolkit. *Proceedings of the 52nd Annual Meeting of the Association for Computational Linguistics: System Demonstrations*, pp. 55–60.

Philip V. Ogren, Guergana K. Savova, and Christopher G. Chute. 2008. Constructing evaluation corpora for automated clinical named entity recognition. *Proceedings of the Language Resources and Evaluation Conference (LREC),* pp. 28–30.

Stelios Piperidis, Dimitrios Galanis, Juli Bakagianni, and Sokratis Sofianopoulos. 2015. Combining and extending data infrastructures with linguistic annotation services. *International Workshop on Worldwide Language Service Infrastructure*, (pp. 3–17). Springer International Publishing.

Xipeng Qiu, Qi Zhang and Xuanjing Huang. 2013. FudanNLP: A Toolkit for Chinese Natural Language Processing. *Proceedings of the 51nd Annual Meeting of the Association for Computational Linguistics: System Demonstrations.*

Ren Speck, and Axel C. N. Ngomo. 2014. Ensemble learning for named entity recognition. *Semantic Web–ISWC 2014. LNCS*, vol 8796, pp. 519–534. Springer, Heidelberg.

Decai Wu, Grace Ngai, and Marine Carpuat. 2003. A stacked, voted, stacked model for named entity recognition. *Proceedings of the Seventh Conference on Natural Language Learning at HLT-NAACL 2003, CONLL 2003*, vol. 4, pp. 200–203. Association for Computational Linguistics, Stroudsburg

Naiwen Xue, Feixia Fu, Dong Chiou, and Marta Palmer. 2005. The Penn Chinese Treebank: Phrase structure annotation of a large corpus. *Natural Language Engineering*, vol. 11, no. 2, pp.207–238.

Zhihua Zhou. 2012. Ensemble methods: foundations and algorithms. *CRC Press*, pp 74–75.

An Ontology for Language Service Composability

Yohei Murakami
Unit of Design,
Kyoto University
yohei@i.kyoto-u.ac.jp

Takao Nakaguchi
Department of Social Informatics
Kyoto University
nakaguchi@i.kyoto-u.ac.jp

Donghui Lin
Department of Social Informatics
Kyoto University
lindh@i.kyoto-u.ac.jp

Toru Ishida
Department of Social Informatics
Kyoto University
ishida@i.kyoto-u.ac.jp

Abstract

Fragmentation and *recombination* is a key to create customized language environments for supporting various intercultural activities. *Fragmentation* provides various language resource components for the customized language environments and *recombination* builds each language environment according to user's request by combining these components. To realize this fragmentation and recombination process, existing language resources (both data and programs) should be shared as language services and combined beyond mismatch of their service interfaces. To address this issue, standardization is inevitable: standardized interfaces are necessary for language services as well as data format required for language resources. Therefore, we have constructed a hierarchy of language services based on inheritance of service interfaces, which is called *language service ontology*. This ontology allows users to create a new customized language service that is compatible with existing ones. Moreover, we have developed a dynamic service binding technology that instantiates various executable customized services from an abstract workflow according to user's request. By using the ontology and service binding together, users can bind the instantiated language service to another abstract workflow for a new customized one.

1 Introduction

Rapid internationalization accelerates expansion of multicultural society where local people and foreigners coexist. As a result, intercultural and multilingual activities are often necessary in daily life, such as questioning foreign patients in hospitals and teaching foreign students in schools, and so on. Although there are many language resources (e.g. bilingual dictionaries, parallel corpora, machine translators, morphological analyzers, and so on) on the Internet(Choukri, 2004), most intercultural collaboration activities are still lacking multilingual support. This is because each activity requires a customized language environment due to different purposes, domains, environments, and languages to be supported.

Many efforts have been put for combining language resources in some previous frameworks based on web services. These efforts focus on wrapping the resources as services, and defining a standard data format exchanged between language services and annotation vocabularies to be embedded in the format. The format and vocabularies enable users to combine language services developed by different providers. However, end users who need multilingual support in their intercultural fields have difficulties in developing a reasonable logic flow to combine language services because they are not familiar with the annotation vocabularies. Therefore, we aim at separating the logic flow from selecting language services by introducing an abstract workflow into our platform. In our platform, web service professionals develop an abstract workflow to combine language services, while users select language services to be

Proceedings of WLSI/OIAF4HLT,
pages 61–69, Osaka, Japan, December 12 2016.

connected by the workflow in order to instantiate their customized language services from the abstract workflow.

To realize this collaboration between web service professionals and end users, we addressed the following two issues.

Construct an ontology to define language services As web service professionals develop new language services according to users' request, it results in generating various service interfaces. To invoke the new services from existing workflows while ensuring the diversity, we need an ontology to verify composability of the new services.

Develop language service binding technology To instantiate various executable composite language services from an abstract workflow, we need a technology that enables users to bind any language services to the workflow when executing the workflow.

The remainder of this paper is organized as follows: in section 2 we will briefly discuss features of the two approaches to combine language services. And then, our framework called *Service Grid* and our proposed *language service ontology* will be presented in section 3 and 4. Moreover, we show how to bridge our language services with ones in different frameworks in section 5. Finally, section 6 concludes this paper.

2   Related Works

There are two types of frameworks supporting developers to combine language resources: pipeline processing approach such as GATE(Cunningham et al., 2002) and UIMA(Ferrucci and Lally, 2004) (U-compare(Kano et al., 2009) and DKPro(Eckart de Castilho and Gurevych, 2014)), and service composition approach such as PANACEA(Toral et al., 2011), LAPPS Grid(Ide et al., 2014), and the Language Grid (Ishida, 2011). The former focuses on processing a huge amount of data at local with pipeline technique. On the other hand, the latter aims to share language resources distributed on the Internet as a web service and combine them in a workflow manner. As shown in Table 1, we summarized features of these frameworks from view point of interfaces, data format, and type system.

2.1   Pipeline Processing Approach

This approach employs a common interfaces and common data format exchanged between language resources. The resources are combined into a pipeline to analyze documents. Each resource called a processing resource or analysis engine annotates a document flowed in the pipeline in the stand-off annotation manner. The document together with annotations is formed in a common data format, such as GATE format and CAS (Common Analysis Structure). The annotations comply with pre-defined annotation type system. GATE provides annotation schemas to define annotation type for each case, while U-Compare and DKPro contain pre-defined annotation types based on UIMA type system.

2.2   Service Composition Approach

This approach wraps language resources as web services, called *language services*, and standardizes the language service interfaces. LAPPS Grid provides a single common method same as the pipeline processing approach, while PANACEA and Language Grid define the interfaces according to language service types because the workflow can freely assign outputs of a service to inputs of another one. The unique feature of this approach is to combine language services distributed in the Internet. This feature requires interoperability of language services on different frameworks. To satisfy this requirement, LAPPS Grid and PANACEA present several format converters between different format and their own formats like LIF (LAPPS Interchange Format)(Verhagen et al., 2016) and Travelling Object. Moreover, LAPPS Grid defines LAPPS Web Service Exchange Vocabulary(Ide et al., 2016), an ontology of terms for a core of linguistic objects and features exchanged among language services that consume and produce linguistically annotated data. It is used for service description and input/output interchange to support service discovery and composition. On the other hand, Language Grid enforces service providers to wrap their resources with the standardized interfaces that expose every annotation data type, in order

Table 1: Comparison among Frameworks

	GATE	U-Compare	DKPro	LAPPS Grid	PANACEA	Language Grid
Standardized Interface	✓ (common)	✓ (common)	✓ (common)	✓ (common)	✓ (each type)	✓ (each type)
Common Format	✓ (GATE format)	✓ (CAS)	✓ (CAS)	✓ (LIF)	✓ (Traveling Object)	
Format Converter				✓	✓	
Type System (Vocabularies)	✓	✓	✓	✓		✓

to remove the needs of a common format and converters. To bridge other service-based frameworks and Language Grid, we have developed adapters that adapt Heart of Gold and UIMA component to our standardized interfaces(Bramantoro et al., 2008; Trang et al., 2014).

The existing frameworks except for the Language Grid combine instances of language services in a pipeline and workflow. The pipeline and workflow that tightly couple language services need to be modified when changing a language service according to user's request. This becomes a barrier for end users to create their customized services by themselves. Therefore, we have introduced an abstract workflow that is composed of interfaces of components and their dependencies. The abstract workflow separates binding language services from designing it so that users can reuse the workflow to instantiate it with combination of language services they want. In this composition method that delays service binding, it is significant to verify which language services are compatible with the designed workflows. Therefore, we describe two ontologies that defines language service type and organizes a hierarchy of language services in section 3 and 4.

3   Service Grid

Interoperability of language services requires standardization of service interfaces and metadata according to their functionalities. To this end, our service grid provides a service grid ontology for operators to organize services in their domain into several service classes (Murakami et al., 2012). As illustrated in Figure 1, the service grid ontology is not just an ontology of data exchanged between services, but an ontology to define service metadata and resource metadata. ServiceGrid class has more than one Resource class and Service class that is provided from the corresponding Resource class. Resource and Service class have more than one attribute to describe features of their instances. Also, Service class has one service interface to allow users to access the service instances via several protocols. A service grid operator can define his domain service grid ontology by inheriting ServiceGrid, Resource, and Service class.

Based on the service grid ontology, we constructed Language Grid Ontology shown in Figure 2. This

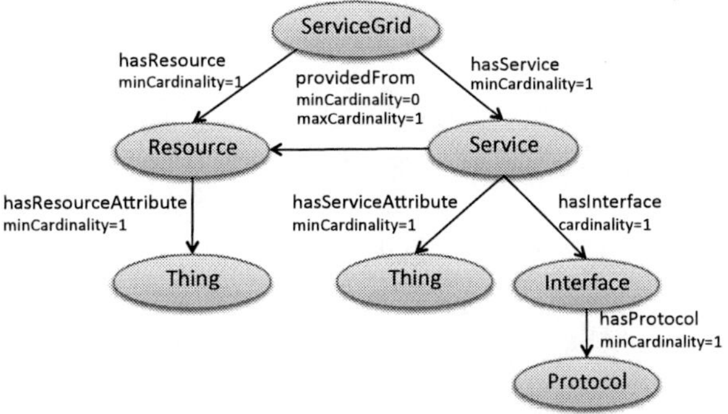

Figure 1: Service Grid Ontology

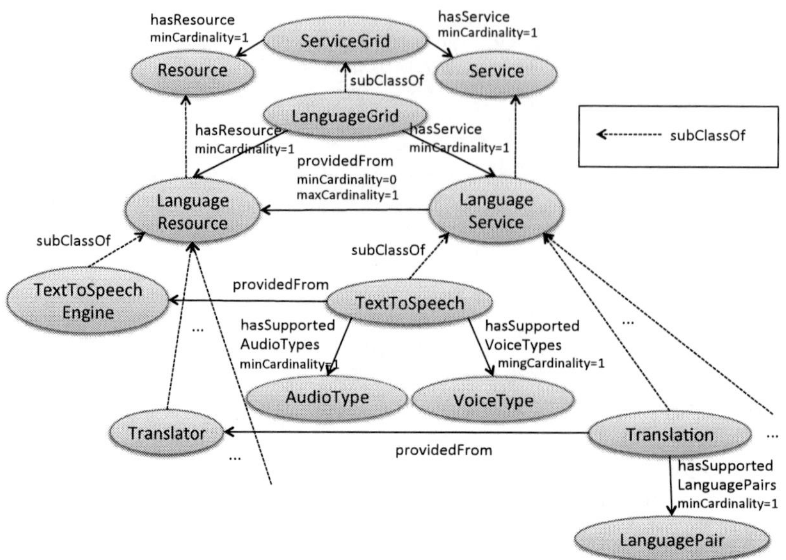

Figure 2: Inheriting Service Grid Ontology

ontology defines LanguageGrid, LanguageResource, and LanguageService classes as subclasses of ServiceGrid, Resource, and Service classes. Moreover, the LanguageResource and LanguageService classes derive 14 types of language resource classes and 17 types of language service classes such as text to speech engines, translator, and so on. Table 2 shows the language service classes. These service classes are characterized with hasServiceAttribute property, indicating which objects a given service can process and which methods the service can employ. The former is *hasSupportedLanguages*, *hasSupportedLanguagePairs*, *hasSupportedLanguagePaths*, *hasSupportedImageTypes*, *hasSupportedAudioTypes*, and *hasSupportedVoiceTypes*. They are used to specify languages, images, and audio files to be processed by services. The latter is *hasSupportedMatchingMethod*. This is used to specify search functionalities implemented on language data such as bilingual dictionaries, concept dictionaries, and so on.

Moreover, we defined a service interface for each service class. To standardize the interface, we extracted common parameters of language resources belonging to the same resource type. In case of morphological analyzers, we have several morphological analysis services according to supported languages: TreeTagger, MeCab, Juman, KLT, ICTCLAS. A source text and source language for input parameters are common among all the existing morphological analyzers. On the other hand, we have many formats of morphemes for output parameters. Every analyzer returns word, lemma, and part of speech tag except for ICTCLAS. Therefore, we defined the output of morphological analysis service as an array of triples consisting of word, lemma, and POS tag. Furthermore, we enumerated POS tags available in the output of the analysis service. Since POS tags vary depending on languages, we selected a minimal set of POS tags occurring in every language: noun, proper noun, pronoun, verb, adjective, adverb, unknown, and other. Most morphological analyzers can be wrapped with this standard interface. A few morphological analyzers not complying with this interface, such as ICTCLAS, return "NULL" as unassigned parameters. This interface is designed for interoperability instead of completeness. As a result, information generated by the original morphological analyzers can be lost.

Due to limitations of space, Table 2 shows only the operation name of Interface class except for input and output parameters. Refer to `http://langrid.org/service_manager/service-type` for the WSDL files and more information. The attributes and interfaces help service users to compose services by searching services with the metadata and changing the services belonging to the same service type.

Table 2: Language Service Classes

Service class	hasServiceAttribute property	Thing class	Interface class
BackTranslation	hasSupportedLanguagePaths	LanguagePath	backtranslate
BilingualDictionary	hasSupportedLanguagePairs, hasSupportedMatchingMethods	LanguagePair, MatchingMethod	search
BilingualDictionaryWith LongestMatchSearch	hasSupportedLanguagePairs, hasSupportedMatchingMethods	LanguagePair, MatchingMethod	search searchWithLongestMatch
ConceptDictionary	hasSupportedLanguages, hasSupportedMatchingMethods	Language, MatchingMethod	searchConcepts, getRelatedConcepts
DependencyParse	hasSupportedLanguages	Language	parseDependency
DialogCorpus	hasSupportedLanguages, hasSupportedMatchingMethods	Language, MatchingMethod	search
LanguageIdentification	hasSupportedEncodings, hasSupportedLanguages	Encoding, Language	identify
MorphologicalAnalysis	hasSupportedLanguages	Language	analyze
MultihopTranslation	hasSupportedLanguagePaths	LanguagePath	translate multihopTranslate
NamedEntityTagging	hasSupportedLanguages	Language	tag
ParallelText	hasSupportedLanguagePairs, hasSupportedMatchingMethods	LanguagePair, MatchingMethod	search
Paraphrase	hasSupportedLanguages	Language	paraphrase
PictogramDictionary	hasSupportedLanguages, hasSupportedMatchingMethods, hasSupportedImageTypes	Language, MatchingMethod, ImageType	search
SimilarityCalculation	hasSupportedLanguages	Language	calculate
SpeechRecognition	hasSupportedLanguages, hasSupportedAudioTypes, hasSupportedVoiceTypes	Language, AudioType, VoiceType	recognize
TextToSpeech	hasSupportedLanguages, hasSupportedAudioTypes, hasSupportedVoiceTypes	Language, AudioType, VoiceType	speak
Translation	hasSupportedLanguagePairs	LanguagePair	translate
TranslationWith TemporalDictionary	hasSupportedLanguagePairs	LanguagePair	translate translateWithDict

4 Language Service Ontology

Service Grid ontology allows operators to add a new service type according to users' requests. As the number of service types increases, the reusability of workflows decreases because the service grid may have many close but not the same interfaces for the common functionalities. For example, when many service users need more detailed information of morphological analysis services, a new one may be added. To increase the reusability of workflows, it is significant to verify which language services are compatible with the existing workflows. In this section, we firstly describe semantic matching that guarantees substitutability of language services in an abstract workflow. Based on the semantic matching, we then construct a hierarchy of language services, and explain how to bind language services to the workflow.

4.1 Semantic Matching

Semantic matching was introduced to discover a service whose capability satisfies user's request(Paolucci et al., 2002). Since the goal of the previous research is to fulfill users' request as much as possible but not partially, the semantic matching prefers services that output a superclass of users' required class. However, our goal is to find services whose capabilities are compatible with the existing workflow. If a service that outputs a superclass of user's required class is selected, the subsequent service in a workflow may fail to run because the service has possibilities to receive an input different from its expected input, such as a sibling class. This semantic matching causes a type-unsafety issue. Therefore, we modify the semantic matching rules by considering type-safety in binding services to a workflow.

Firstly, we define notations relevant to an input-output of a service, and then modify the semantic matching rules.

Definition 4.1 (Input-output of a service) *A service s is defined as a tuple $s = \{Input_s, Output_s\} \in S$ where $Input_s$ is a set of inputs required to invoke s, $Output_s$ is the set of outputs returned by s after its execution, and S is the set of all services registered in a service grid. Each input and output is also a*

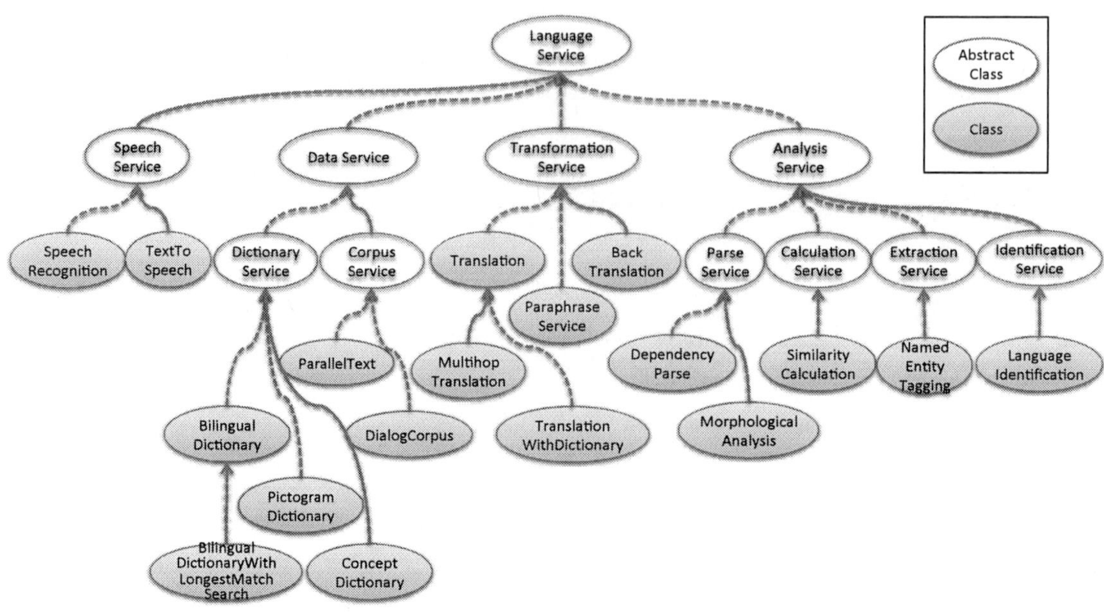

Figure 3: Language Service Ontology

class.

Exact An input $i_s \in Input_s$ and an output $o_s \in Output_s$ of a service s in a set of services S matches an input $i_w \in Input_w$ and output $o_w \in Output_w$ of a service w in a workflow with a degree of exact match if both of input and output classes are equivalent ($i_s \equiv i_w, o_s \equiv o_w$).

Plug-in An input $i_s \in Input_s$ and an output $o_s \in Output_s$ of a service s in a set of services S matches an input $i_w \in Input_w$ and an output $o_w \in Output_w$ of a service w in a workflow with a degree of plugin if i_s is a superclass of i_w ($i_s \sqsupseteq i_w$) and o_s is a subclass of o_w ($o_s \sqsubseteq o_w$).

Subsume An input $i_s \in Input_s$ and an output $o_s \in Output_s$ of a service s in a set of services S matches an input $i_w \in Input_w$ and an output $o_w \in Output_w$ of a service w in a workflow with a degree of subsume if either i_s is a subclass of i_w ($i_s \sqsubset i_w$) or o_s is a superclass of o_w ($o_s \sqsupset o_w$).

Fail When none of the previous matches are found, then both concepts are incompatible and the match has a degree of fail.

Note that, in order to discover type safe services to satisfy data flow in a workflow execution, the only two valid degrees of match are *exact* and *plug-in*. Based on the *exact* match, the Language Grid has introduced inheritance of service interfaces, which guarantees that an inherited interface provides the same methods as the superclass of a service. We construct a hierarchy of language services using the inheritance of service interfaces in 4.2

4.2 Hierarchy of Language Services

When many service users need more additional detailed information, a new service class can be derived by inheriting the service interface of the superclass, but not created from scratch. The inherited service interface can add other interfaces while maintaining the consistency with the existing one. This inheritance of service interfaces constructs a hierarchy of homogeneous services. This is similar to a OWL-S profile hierarchy(Martin et al., 2007) and WSMO capability(Wang et al., 2012). However, they are used to discover alternative services from property aspect but not interfaces like existing taxonomies of service categories.

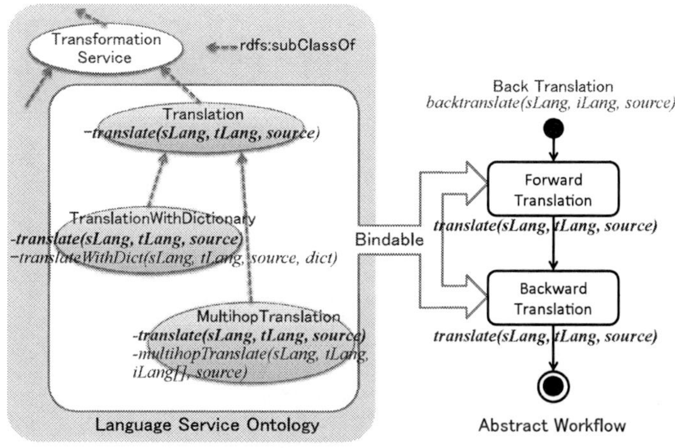

Figure 4: Service Binding with Language Service Ontology

Figure 3 illustrates our hierarchy of language services based on interface inheritance, called *Language Service Ontology*. This ontology consists of abstract classes that have no interface and instance of services and classes that have interfaces and instances. Firstly, LanguageService class is classified into four abstract classes: SpeechService class that processes speech data, DataService class that deals with linguistic data resources like lexical and corpus data, TransformationService class that transforms input texts, and AnalysisService class that analyzes input data like parsing, calculating, extracting, and identifying. By inheriting the abstract classes, we define 18 language service classes listed in Table 2.

Moreover, MultihopTranslation and TranslationWithDictionary class, and BilingualDictionaryWith-LongestMatchSearch class are derived from Translation class and BilingualDictionary class, respectively. Hence, they have the same interface as their superclass. For example, as shown in the left side of Figure 4, Translation class provides a translate method whose input parameters are source language, target language, and source text (denoted by sLang, tLang, source, respectively). By extending this interface, TranslationWithDictionary and MultihopTranslation class are defined as a subclass of Translation class. The former introduces simple dictionary data into its input parameters in order to replace words in the translated text with translated words in the dictionary. This aims at improving translation quality by restricting context within the dictionary. Without the dictionary, this service returns a translated text like Translation class. On the other hand, the latter introduces an array of intermediate languages to cascade several translation services. Without intermediate languages, this service behaves like Translation class by using default languages as intermediate languages.

Based on this ontology, we can bind any subclasses to an abstract workflow including the superclass's interface. The right side of Figure 4 shows the case of backtranslation. This workflow connects two translation interfaces to translate the translated text into the source language again. Therefore, we can select JServer, an instance of Translation class, and DictTrans, an instance of TranslationWithDictionary, as a forward translation and backward translation, respectively. To dynamically bind these services in invoking the backtranslation service, we have introduced a hierarchical service composition description using higher-order functions as below(Nakaguchi et al., 2016). This syntax allows users to nest binding in order to invoke a workflow from another one.

```
syntax  :== service "." method "(" (arg ("," arg)* )? ")"
service :== serviceId | serviceBinding
method  :== symbol
serviceId :== symbol
serviceBinding :== "bind(" serviceId bindingInfo+ ")"
bindingInfo :== "," invocationId ":" service
invocationId :== symbol
arg :== "'" symbol "'"
symbol  :== LETTER+
```

Using this language, we can describe the above service binding as below. After executing this language, this description is translated into a SOAP request embedding the binding information into the header.

```
bind(BackTranslation,
 ForwardTranslation:JServer,
 BackwardTranslation:bind(DictTrans,
  MorphologicalAnalysis:TreeTagger,
  BilingualDictionary:AgriDict,
  Translation:GoogleTranslate
 ).backtranslate('en','ja','Land preparation needs puddling and levee painting.')
```

5   Discussion

Our language service ontology focuses on interoperability among homogeneous language services. Meanwhile, it is also significant to enhance interoperability among heterogenous language services. We have two approaches.

One is to construct central ontology as a hub, which was proposed by (Hayashi et al., 2008). The ontology consists of a top-level ontology and sub-ontologies. The top-level ontology defines the relations among language service class, language processing resource class, language data resource class, and linguistic object class. A language service is provided by an instance of the language processing resource class, whose input and output are instances of linguistic object class. A language data resource consists of instances of the linguistic object class. On the other hand, each sub-ontology organizes classes for language processing resources, language data resources, and linguistic annotations of linguistic objects, respectively.

The other is to connect type systems in different frameworks each other. By mapping LAPPS exchange vocabulary type hierarchy and type system in DKPro and U-Compare with input and output classes of language service interfaces in our ontology, it would be possible to discover type safe services with *plug-in* match as well as *exact* match. Logically, covariant return type of services, which return a subclass of the output class, and contravariant argument type of services, which receive a superclass of the input class can be bindable to an abstract workflow.

6   Conclusions

We have introduced an abstract workflow to separate designing a logic flow and selecting language services. By this abstract workflow, we aim at realizing collaboration between web service professionals who develop a workflow and end users who select their needed language services. To this end, we have constructed language service ontology by inheriting service interfaces to verify composability of language services. Moreover, we have applied higher-order function to develop hierarchical language service binding. By using the ontology and binding technology, end users can instantiate an abstract workflow with type-safe language services.

Acknowledgements

This work was supported by Grant-in-Aid for Scientific Research (S) (24220002) of Japan Society for the Promotion of Science (JSPS).

References

Arif Bramantoro, Masahiro Tanaka, Yohei Murakami, Ulrich Schäfer, and Toru Ishida. 2008. A Hybrid Integrated Architecture for Language Service Composition. In *Proc. of the Sixth International Conference on Web Services (ICWS'08)*, pages 345–352.

Khalid Choukri. 2004. European Language Resources Association History and Recent Developments. In *SCALLA Working Conference KC 14/20*.

Hamish Cunningham, Diana Maynard, Kalina Bontcheva, and Valentin Tablan. 2002. GATE: An Architecture for Development of Robust HLT Applications. In *Proc. of the Fortieth Annual Meeting on Association for Computational Linguistics (ACL'02)*, pages 168–175.

Richard Eckart de Castilho and Iryna Gurevych. 2014. A Broad-Coverage Collection of Portable NLP Components for Building Shareable Analysis Pipelines. In *Proceedings of the Workshop on Open Infrastructures and Analysis Frameworks for HLT*, pages 1–11.

David Ferrucci and Adam Lally. 2004. UIMA: An Architectural Approach to Unstructured Information Processing in the Corporate Research Environment. *Journal of Natural Language Engineering*, 10:327–348.

Yoshihiko Hayashi, Thierry Declerck, Paul Buitelaar, and Monica Monachini. 2008. Ontologies for a Global Language Infrastructure. In *Proc. of the First International Conference on Global Interoperability for Language Resources (ICGL'08)*, pages 105–112.

Nancy Ide, James Pustejovsky, Christopher Cieri, Eric Nyberg, Di Wang, Keith Suderman, Marc Verhagen, and Jonathan Wright. 2014. The Language Application Grid. In *Proceedings of the Ninth International Conference on Language Resources and Evaluation (LREC'14)*, pages 22–30.

Nancy Ide, Keith Suderman, Marc Verhagen, and James Pustejovsky. 2016. The Language Application Grid Web Service Exchange Vocabulary. In *Worldwide Language Service Infrastructure*, pages 18–32. Springer International Publishing.

Toru Ishida, editor. 2011. *The Language Grid: Service-Oriented Collective Intelligence for Language Resource Interoperability*. Springer-Verlag.

Yoshinobu Kano, William Baumgartner, Luke McCrohon, Sophia Ananiadou, Kevin Cohen, Larry Hunter, and Jun'ichi Tsujii. 2009. U-Compare: Share and Compare Text Mining Tools with UIMA. *Bioinformatics*, 25(15):1997–1998.

David Martin, Mark Burstein, Drew McDermott, Sheila McIlraith, Massimo Paolucci, Katia Sycara, Deborah L. McGuinness, Evren Sirin, and Naveen Srinivasan. 2007. Bringing Semantics to Web Services with OWL-S. *World Wide Web*, 10(3):243–277.

Yohei Murakami, Masahiro Tanaka, Donghui Lin, and Toru Ishida. 2012. Service Grid Federation Architecture for Heterogeneous Domains. In *Proc. of the IEEE International Conference on Services Computing (SCC-12)*, pages 539–546.

Takao Nakaguchi, Yohei Murakami, Donghui Lin, and Toru Ishida. 2016. Higher-Order Functrions for Modeling Hierarchical Service Bindings. In *Proc. of the Twelfth International Conference on Web Services (ICWS'08)*, pages 798–803.

Massimo Paolucci, Takahiro Kawamura, Terry R. Payne, and Katia Sycara. 2002. Semantic Matching of Web Services Capabilities. In *Proc. of the First International Semantic Web Conference (ISWC'02)*, pages 333–347.

Antonio Toral, Pavel Pecina, Andy Way, and Marc Poch. 2011. Towards a User-Friendly Webservice Architecture for Statistical Machine Translation in the PANACEA Project. In *Proc. of the 15th Conference of the European Association for Machine Translation (EAMT'11)*, pages 63–70.

Mai Xuan Trang, Yohei Murakami, Donghui Lin, and Toru Ishida. 2014. Integration of Workflow and Pipeline for Language Service Composition. In *Proc. of the 9th International Conference on Language Resources and Evaluation Conference (LREC'14)*, pages 3829–3836.

Marc Verhagen, Keith Suderman, Di Wang, Nancy Ide, Chunqi Shi, Jonathan Wright, and James Pustejovsky. 2016. The LAPPS Interchange Format. In *Worldwide Language Service Infrastructure*, pages 33–47. Springer International Publishing.

Hai H. Wang, Nick Gibbins, Terry R. Payne, and Domenico Redavid. 2012. A Formal Model of the Semantic Web Service Ontology (WSMO). *Information Systems*, 37(1):33–60.

Between Platform and APIs: Kachako API for Developers

Yoshinobu Kano
Faculty of Informatics, Shizuoka University, Japan
`kano@inf.shizuoka.ac.jp`

Abstract

Different types of users require different functions in NLP software. It is difficult for a single platform to cover all types of users. When a framework aims to provide more interoperability, users are required to learn more concepts; users' application designs are restricted to be compliant with the framework. While an interoperability framework is useful in certain cases, some types of users will not select the framework due to the learning cost and design restrictions. We suggest a rather simple framework for the interoperability aiming at developers. Reusing an existing NLP platform Kachako, we created an API oriented NLP system. This system loosely couples rich high-end functions, including annotation visualizations, statistical evaluations, annotation searching, etc. This API do not require users much learning cost, providing customization ability for power users while also allowing easy users to employ many GUI functions.

1   Introduction

A platform type of NLP software tends to provide rich GUI functions for easy users to help avoiding burdensome tasks that are not essential for their purposes. However, power users require customization ability in an API oriented way. There has been many efforts to create interoperable NLP systems, including GATE (Cunningham et al., 2002), Taverna (Hull et al., 2006), Galaxy (Blankenberg et al., 2010), Langrid (Ishida, 2006), Heart of Gold (Schäfer, 2006), PANACEA (Bel, 2010), etc.

UIMA (Unstructured Information Management Architecture) is an interoperability framework originally developed by IBM (Ferrucci et al., 2006), currently an open source project in Apache UIMA[2]. Most of UIMA related works are UIMA component implementations, including OpenNLP, JulieLab (Hahn et al., 2008), CCP BioNLP (Baumgartner Jr. et al., 2008), U-Compare (Kano et al., 2009), UIMA-fr (Hernandez et al., 2010), DKPro (Müller et al., 2008), cTAKES (Savova et al., 2010), etc.

Among the UIMA based systems, Kachako (Kano, 2012b) provides many generic features useful for developers to analyze and improve their applications. Unfortunately, these features are parts of a large integrated system which are not easy for the developers to partially reuse. Furthermore, certain number of developers avoid learning UIMA due to UIMA's rich but complex higher interoperability concepts.

We suggest a simplified interface that just requires the so-called stand-off annotation style data structure. In order for developers to more easily reuse Kachako's features, we built an API oriented NLP system based on Kachako, changing to the simplified interface discarding its UIMA compliancy.

We describe points of the UIMA framework (Section 2), the features of the Kachako platform (Section 3), and our suggested simple framework with actual API oriented system (Section 4), finally concluding this paper (Section 5).

2   UIMA

We introduce the basic architecture of UIMA briefly in this section. We refer to the Java implementation of Apache UIMA as UIMA here.

A tool is represented as a *component* in UIMA. A component is a processing unit of UIMA. In UIMA, components are combined in a *workflow*. Processing order of components can be programmable, while most workflows are simple pipelines. UIMA's data structure, *CAS (Common Analysis Structure)*, is in the so-called stand-off format, which consists of a raw (text) data part and an annotation part. The Java version of CAS is called *JCas*. An annotation should be typed by a *type system*, a user defined type

---

[2] http://uima.apache.org/

Proceedings of WLSI/OIAF4HLT,
pages 70–75, Osaka, Japan, December 12 2016.

hierarchy. A component receives a CAS, may update the CAS and returns the CAS. A component may
have its input and output types specified. These types are defined in a UIMA's type system descriptor
XML file by the user. Each type is also defined in a corresponding Java class. Basically, CAS should
include everything in UIMA. A CAS has one or more *sofa* (Subject OF Analysis, or sometimes called
view) to hold multi-modal information such as text and audio, original and translated text, etc.

As a whole, in order to use UIMA for combining various NLP tools, researchers should create workflows for combining tools and define types for connecting the input and output of these tools. When
running a UIMA workflow, users normally use UIMA's workflow API where CAS creation and disposal
are controlled by the UIMA framework side, not by Java VM. A CAS is passed from component to
component, then disposed from the Java heap memory after returned by a final component of a workflow.
Therefore, developers need to pay attention not to hold any reference to content of a CAS after the CAS
finished a workflow, else memory leak occurs even this is a Java API. Its reason is explained as an
efficient memory usage by the Apache UIMA documentation. This makes a pitfall to developers.

3   Kachako Platform

The Kachako platform aims to provide automation features on top of the UIMA framework (Kano,
2012a)(Kano, 2012b). If the users can complete their tasks by GUI operations, most UIMA things are
obscured in Kachako. However, users are required knowledge of some UIMA concepts.

Roughly speaking, Kachako has four features: automatic workflow creation, automatic workflow execution, Annotation Viewer GUI for result analysis with statistical table for comparison and evaluation,
Annotation Searcher to index and search the results. We explain each feature below.

As Kachako aims to provide automation features, installation, update and execution of the platform
itself is automatic in a web-based way. Kachako has its tens of own UIMA components that are also
ready-to-use by automatic installation feature. Users can also register their own UIMA components to
create a UIMA workflow using these UIMA components. Users can create a UIMA workflow automatically or manually by selecting UIMA components. Figure 1 shows the Kachako's workflow creation
GUI. Each round-bordered box corresponds to a UIMA component, which input ports are shown in the
right, output ports are shown in the right. These I/O ports are specific to Kachako, which ensures connections between components. The automatic workflow creation feature uses these I/O information to
calculate (partial) workflow candidates when a start component and an end component are specified by
users. These ports may belong to different sofas, shown as thick coloured labels in Figure 1. Each component may have configuration parameters, whose setting panel is available in this GUI.

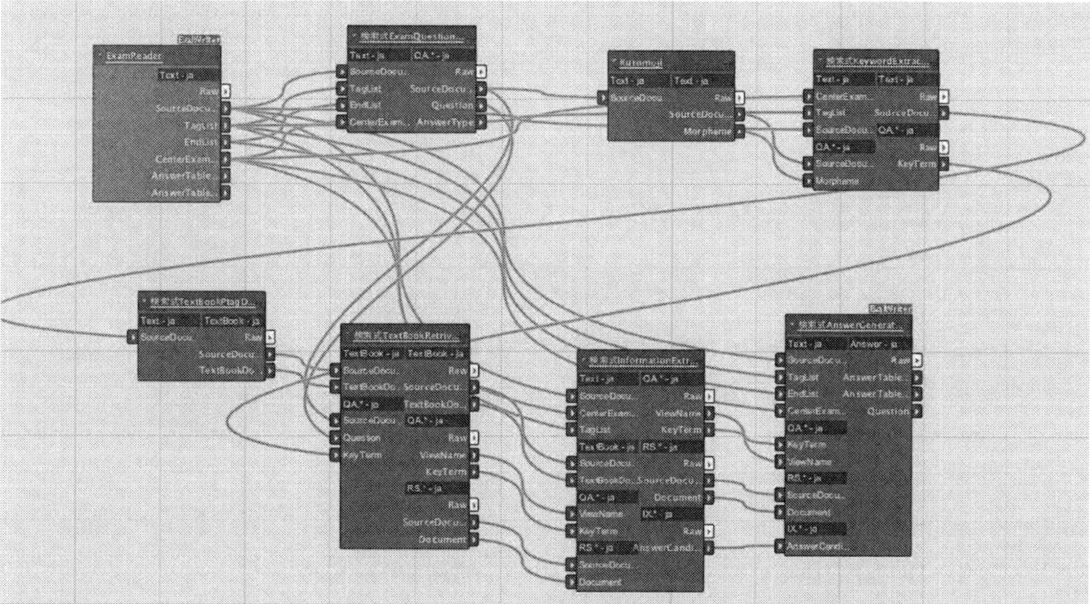

Figure 1. A screenshot of workflow creation GUI. This complex example shows a workflow of the
History examination solver for the Todai Robot project (Kano, 2014).

Once a workflow is created, installation and execution of the workflow and its components are available automatically. As this is a UIMA workflow, workflow results are stored as CASes. Figure 2 shows a screenshot of the Annotation Viewer GUI that fully visualizes contents of a CAS. The leftmost panel shows the visualization result where each annotation is displayed as an underline with the raw text part. Users can filter which annotation types to show in the middle panel. The rightmost panel shows all of field values of annotations in a sortable way. Users can select a specific annotation to jump and highlight.

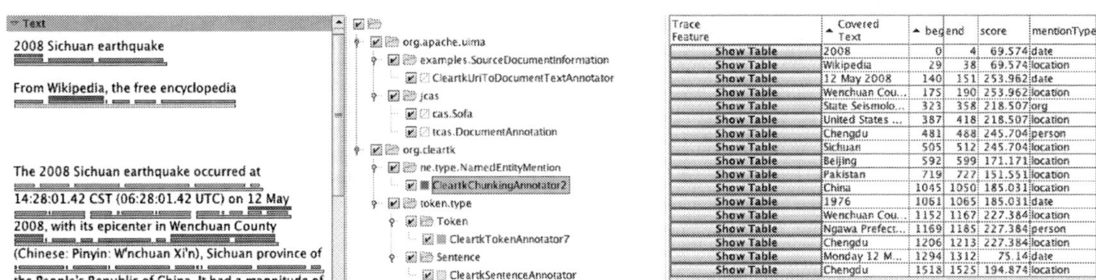

Figure 2. A screenshot of Annotation Viewer GUI.

Kachako has a comparison and evaluation feature where users can plug their own evaluation metrics as UIMA components. Figure 3 shows an example of a comparison workflow. Purple boxes in the right are evaluation components that receives a pair of input ports of same type, performs comparisons.

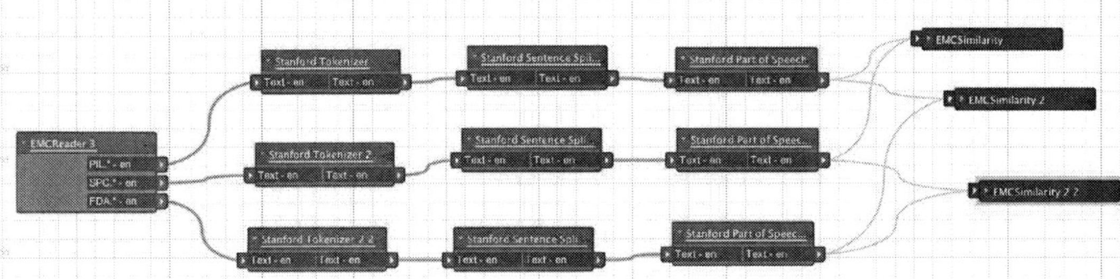

Figure 3. A screenshot of a comparison/evaluation workflow.

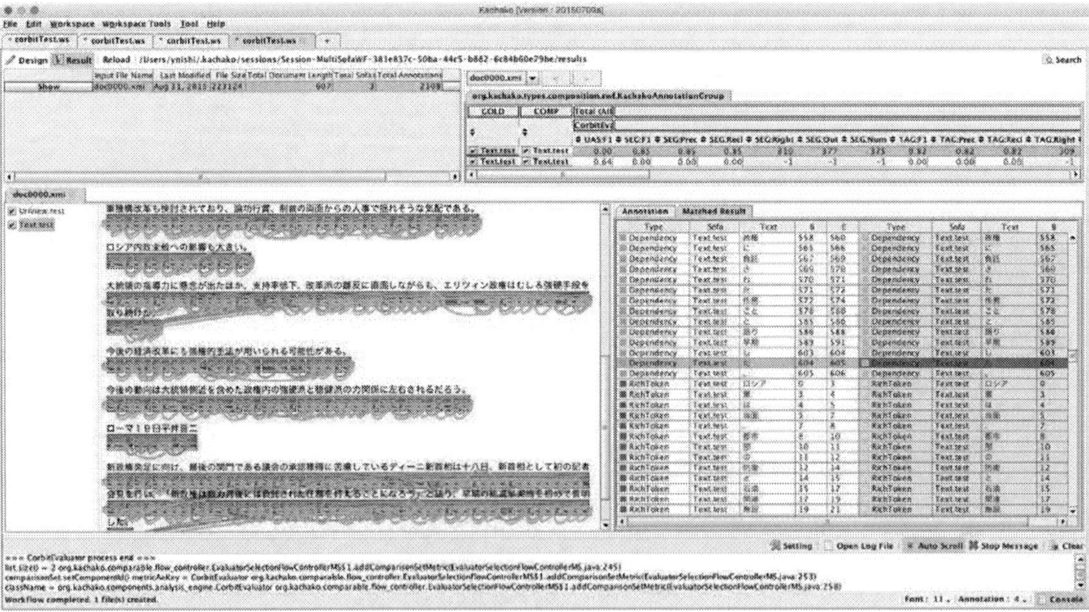

Figure 4. A screenshot of the Annotation Viewer for a comparison/evaluation workflow.

Figure 4 shows a result window of such an evaluation workflow. The upper-left panel shows statistics for each CAS, e.g. numbers of annotations. The upper-right panel shows statistics of evaluation metrics, e.g. precision, recall, and F-score while these metrics could be customized as shown in the figure. Comparison/evaluation components should be implemented by developers as there could be variety of different metrics depending on the individual developers' purposes. The lower-left panel is the Annotation Viewer, while sofa selector is shown in the left as this is a multi-sofa case. The Annotation Viewer shows rather a complex example, where many inter-annotation links are shown as arcs. The lower-right panel shows the feature values of annotations. Users can also highlight which specific annotation was matched with respect to a given metric.

Annotation Searcher is an optional function in Kachako to enable indexing and searching of CAS contents. As the example screenshots illustrate, annotations could be very complex, whose number can be huge. It is not realistic to manually check interested patterns of annotations. However, existing search engines assume to index textual information and simple values in their default. Annotation Searcher provides a special function to search by region algebra (Clarke et al., 1995)(Jaakkola et al., 1999)(Masuda et al., 2009) which can cover most of required complex queries, including AND/OR operators, inter-annotation relationships of overlap, follow, include, etc., and inter-annotation links while mixing with the normal textual search conditions. The Annotation Searcher is built on top of Apache Solr/Lucece[3] search engine, adding this region algebra feature in an efficient way, allowing automatic parallel indexing/searching. The Annotation Searcher can be called by just checking an option, receiving any CAS content to index its text and annotations. Search result can be shown in the Annotation Viewer to highlight corresponding annotations.

4   Simplified Interoperability and Kachako API

We suggest a simplified interface for interoperability in order for the developers to more easily employ the functions of Kachako platform. We built an API version of Kachako based on this interface.

Firstly, we discard functions related to the workflow construction. Discarded functions include the automatic workflow creation and its GUI.

Secondly, we designed a pseudo JCas interface which is similar to the original UIMA JCas but just a normal Java class. This pseudo JCas has a text part and an annotations part as same as the original JCas. The annotations part assumes to hold instances of a pseudo *TOP* type or descendants we define. That is, the original type system is defined as a Java class hierarchy. Developers are simply required to produce this pseudo JCas to use the Kachako API functions.

By these designs, we could reuse the Kachako platform functions without much changes. Most of the functions are now available as API by these changes. For example, if developers generate any pseudo JCas, they can simply call the Annotation Searcher API to index and search the content of the pseudo JCas. The Annotation Viewer GUI is available just reading the pseudo JCas. The comparison and evaluation features of the Annotation Viewer GUI is also available by storing groups of annotations.

Modifying existing components into this simplified API is straightforward, because we used similar names for corresponding classes and methods. We discarded the original JCas's index feature, because the pseudo JCas could be extended to store any field, while the annotations part could be used as the original indexed annotations. We have already modified a couple of Kachako UIMA components into this new interface style, which simply required to change several lines of codes per component.

5   Conclusion and Future Work

Interoperability framework is useful but we need different level of interfaces depending on the types of users. UIMA provides a good framework for NLP users but it also restricts users' design due to its workflow management system. Kachako, a UIMA based NLP platform, also suffers the same problem just because it is compliant with UIMA. We build a new API oriented system reusing the Kachako platform, where the interoperability interface is simplified to be only stand-off annotations. This new system allows developers to use its functions without learning costs. Future work includes a new feature to employ machine learning features.

---

[3] https://lucene.apache.org/

Acknowledgement

This work was partially supported by MEXT Kakenhi.

Reference

Baumgartner Jr., W. A., Cohen, K. B. and Hunter, L. (2008). An open-source framework for large-scale, flexible evaluation of biomedical text mining systems. *J Biomed Discov Collab*, *3*(1), 1. Journal Article, . doi:1747-5333-3-1 [pii]10.1186/1747-5333-3-1

Bel, N. (2010). Platform for automatic, normalized annotation and cost-effective acquisition of language resources for human language technologies. panacea. *Procesamiento del Lenguaje Natural*, *45*, 327–328. article, .

Blankenberg, D., Von Kuster, G., Coraor, N., Ananda, G., Lazarus, R., Mangan, M., Nekrutenko, A. and Taylor, J. (2010). Galaxy: a web-based genome analysis tool for experimentalists. *Curr Protoc Mol Biol, Chapter 19*, Unit 19 10 1-21. Journal Article, . doi:10.1002/0471142727.mb1910s89

Clarke, C. L. A., Cormack, G. V. and Burkowski, F. J. (1995). An Algebra for Structured Text Search and a Framework for its Implementation. *The Computer Journal*, *38*(1), 43–56. doi:10.1093/comjnl/38.1.43

Cunningham, H., Maynard, D., Bontcheva, K. and Tablan, V. (2002). GATE: A framework and graphical development environment for robust NLP tools and applications. *40th Anniversary Meeting of the Association for Computational Linguistics* (pp. 168–175). Conference Proceedings, Philadelphia, USA.

Ferrucci, D., Lally, A., Gruhl, D., Epstein, E., Schor, M., Murdock, J. W., Frenkiel, A., Brown, E. W., Hampp, T., et al. (2006). Towards an Interoperability Standard for Text and Multi-Modal Analytics. Report, IBM Research Report.

Hahn, U., Buyko, E., Landefeld, R., Mühlhausen, M., Poprat, M., Tomanek, K. and Wermter, J. (2008). An Overview of JCoRe, the JULIE Lab UIMA Component Repository. *LREC '08 Workshop, Towards Enhanced Interoperability for Large HLT Systems: UIMA for NLP* (pp. 1–8). Conference Proceedings, Marrakech, Morocco.

Hernandez, N., Poulard, F., Vernier, M. and Rocheteau, J. (2010). Building a French-speaking community around UIMA, gathering research, education and industrial partners, mainly in Natural Language Processing and Speech Recognizing domains. *LREC 2010 Workshop of New Challenges for NLP Frameworks*. Conference Proceedings, Valletta, Malta.

Hull, D., Wolstencroft, K., Stevens, R., Goble, C., Pocock, M. R., Li, P. and Oinn, T. (2006). Taverna: a tool for building and running workflows of services. *Nucleic Acids Res*, *34*(Web Server issue), W729-32. Journal Article, . doi:34/suppl_2/W729 [pii]10.1093/nar/gkl320

Ishida, T. (2006). Language Grid: An Infrastructure for Intercultural Collaboration. *Proceedings of the International Symposium on Applications on Internet*. Conference Paper, IEEE Computer Society. doi:10.1109/saint.2006.40

Jaakkola, J. and Kilpeläinen, P. (1999). *Nested Text-Region Algebra* (techreport).

Kano, Y. (2012b). Kachako: a Hybrid-Cloud Unstructured Information Platform for Full Automation of Service Composition, Scalable Deployment and Evaluation. *the 1st International Workshop on Analytics Services on the Cloud (ASC), the 10th International Conference on Services Oriented Computing (ICSOC 2012)*. Shanghai, China.

Kano, Y. (2012a). Towards automation in using multi-modal language resources: compatibility and interoperability for multi-modal features in Kachako. *The Eighth edition of the International Conference on Language Resources and Evaluation (LREC 2012)*. Istanbul, Turkey.

Kano, Y. (2014). Solving History Exam by Keyword Distribution: KJP System at NTCIR-11 QALab Task. *the 11th NTCIR (NII Testbeds and Community for information access Research) workshop* (pp. 530–531).

Kano, Y., Baumgartner, W. A., McCrohon, L., Ananiadou, S., Cohen, K. B., Hunter, L. and Tsujii, J. (2009). U-Compare: share and compare text mining tools with UIMA. *Bioinformatics*, *25*(15), 1997–1998. Journal Article, . doi:10.1093/bioinformatics/btp289

Masuda, K. and Tsujii, J. (2009). Tag-Annotated Text Search Using Extended Region Algebra. *IEICE Transactions on Information and Systems*, *E92.D*(12), 2369–2377. article, . doi:10.1587/transinf.E92.D.2369

Müller, C., Zesch, T., Müller, M.-C., Bernhard, D., Ignatova, K., Gurevych, I. and Mühlhäuser, M. (2008). Flexible UIMA Components for Information Retrieval Research. *LREC 2008 Workshop "Towards Enhanced Interoperability for Large HLT Systems: UIMA for NLP"* (pp. 24–27). Conference Proceedings, Marrakech, Morocco.

Savova, G. K., Masanz, J. J., Ogren, P. V, Zheng, J., Sohn, S., Kipper-Schuler, K. C. and Chute, C. G. (2010). Mayo clinical Text Analysis and Knowledge Extraction System (cTAKES): architecture, component evaluation and applications. *Journal of the American Medical Informatics Association : JAMIA*, *17*(5), 507–13. BMJ Publishing Group Ltd. doi:10.1136/jamia.2009.001560

Schäfer, U. (2006). Middleware for creating and combining multi-dimensional NLP markup. *Proceedings of the 5th Workshop on NLP and XML: Multi-Dimensional Markup in Natural Language Processing*, NLPXML '06 (pp. 81–84). inproceedings, Stroudsburg, PA, USA: Association for Computational Linguistics. Retrieved from http://dl.acm.org/citation.cfm?id=1621034.1621050

Author Index